SOU'WEST AND BY WEST OF CAPE COD

The classic evocation of New England shore, sea, and islands — from Point Judith to the head of Buzzards Bay.

by Llewellyn Howland

Introduction by John Rousmaniere
Illustrations by Lois Darling

YANKEE BOOKS

A division of Yankee Publishing Incorporated
Dublin, New Hampshire

Designed by Jill Shaffer

Yankee Publishing Incorporated
Dublin, New Hampshire
First Edition. Second Printing, 1988.
Copyright 1987 by Yankee Books

Library of Congress Cataloging-in-Publication Data

Howland, Llewellyn.
    Sou'west and by west of Cape Cod.

    (A Yankee classic)
    Reprint. Originally published: Cambridge, Mass. :
Harvard University Press, 1947.
    1. Buzzards Bay Region (Mass. : Bay) — Social life and
customs.   2. New Bedford (Mass.) — Social life and cus-
toms.   3. Howland, Llewellyn — Childhood and youth.
4. Buzzards Bay Region (Mass. : Bay) —Biography.   5. New
Bedford (Mass.) — Biography.   I. Title.
F72.B9H6 1987   974.4'8   87-2094
ISBN 0-89909-142-3

Contents

Foreword

SOME TWENTY-ONE years ago I was both elated and depressed on learning that a boy had been born who, God willing, would in time come to call me "Grandpa." The dual emotions evoked by this event were surprising in that, while I looked forward with youthful eagerness to the days when this newcomer might become my playmate, I was also shockingly aware that the hilltops I had been climbing toward heretofore had suddenly leveled off, with the grade ahead now tending downward instead of upward.

Here was a crisis in which I had no precedent to guide me. And so, as I suspect all others in like case have done and will do, I did nothing more than let Nature take her course; with the result that time passed and other boys, and girls, in this same category arrived to diffuse my solicitude and accustom me to the relationship, I began to act the role of Grandpa with a very real sense of inadequacy — but without undue self-consciousness or repining, even when I found my joints too stiff to respond with enthusiasm and grace to invitations to run, jump, and climb.

Then came a day when I discovered that first-born grandson eagerly reading an article in a popular magazine which dealt lengthily and erroneously with a matter near to my heart: the preparation of that ancient New England rite, the clambake — whereat my foggy conception of how to play the part of grandfather was replaced by the conviction that hereafter I could be both a more entertaining and acceptable playmate and an inspiring mentor by presenting my youthful self in appropriate surroundings by means of the written word.

5

Thus it was that my own "Tales of a Grandfather" took shape without thought of an audience beyond our family circle; until an old friend, Roger L. Scaife, having read my rebuttal to what I considered the half-baked description of a clambake, brought it to the attention of an editor, Edward Weeks, who courageously published it in his own magazine, the *Atlantic Monthly.*

Since then, as other tales of mine have appeared in the *Atlantic,* the *Rudder,* and the *New Bedford Standard-Times,* I have been repaid a thousandfold for the labor involved in writing them — for words do not flow easily from my pen onto paper — by many evidences of interest and approval from friends and hitherto strangers, both old and young.

And now that Roger Scaife has once again confirmed his interest in my articles recalling events and scenes of long ago, by collecting and publishing several of them in book form under the imprint of the Harvard University Press, I take this opportunity to acknowledge with sincerest thanks the help and encouragement that both he and Edward Weeks have most generously given me; and at the same time to convey my gratitude to Miss Mercy E. Baker of New Bedford for interpreting, correcting, and typing my handwritten manuscripts; and finally, but by no means least, to acknowledge my indebtedness to Mrs. Louis MacIntyre Darling for the illustrations embellishing this book, and to all those members, both known and unknown, of the staffs of publishers, who by their professional skill have so faithfully reproduced in type what I have written.

L.H.
February, 1947

Introduction

W ITH THE average sort of book, the special appeal usually does not surface for ten or twenty pages. This cannot be said of *Sou'West and By West of Cape Cod*. Here, the opening sentence confronts the reader with a charm that does not fade for nearly two hundred pages. While setting the scene for his memoirs of a boyhood on a New England salt-water farm in around 1900, Llewellyn Howland confesses right out that he can love, "with that fervor which stirs the very clay of my bones, but one small region in this wide world." After regarding this candid admission, anybody who snaps shut the covers and shoves the book back on the shelf deserves our pity, for only a displaced, cold heart lives without a favorite "small region in this wide world," whether in reality or in dreams.

The warp and the woof of this small masterpiece of regional writing are just those dreams and realities of a lifelong love affair with a place and a time. The enchanting fourteen stories in *Sou'West and By West of Cape Cod* cover a vast territory of experience — late night rides, Menemsha Indian legends, going after bluefish, human relations between the generations, a yacht race, a traditional Christmas — but their terrain is limited to a concretely real and lovingly presented "small region." This place is the shore and waters of Buzzards Bay, which curves between the Massachusetts mainland, to the west, and Cape Cod, the Elizabeth Islands, and Martha's Vineyard. The sounds, smells, and natural phenomena of the bay leap from these pages from the moment that Howland begins to travel in memory down the country lane he calls the "Middle Road" toward the farmhouse of his mentor, "the Skipper," where awaits a boyhood that approaches perfection.

As faithful as these writings are to their place, this stroll into the past is much more than a realistic description of a geographical setting, for *Sou'West and By West of Cape Cod* evokes moods — simplicity, self-sufficiency, friendship, good cheer — as readily as it sketches pictures. The remarkable success of this overlapping of fact and feel is due, in part, to Howland's delicious style, which combines masterful descriptive writing (for example, the traditional New England recipes scattered through the text and the thrilling race of Chapter Eight) with a wealth of imagery and assonance, which pays off wonderfully when the book is read aloud.

The book's mood is also a product of the limits that Howland imposes on his memories. Like much writing that is put in the category of nostalgia, this book succeeds as much in what the author chose *not* to write about as in what he included. Writing in the late 1930s and early 1940s, Howland chose to be selective in his memories of what Buzzards Bay was like between about 1890 and 1910. His highly idealized geography consists almost entirely of quiet harbors filled with sail-driven commercial and pleasure boats and, on the peninsulas that separated one port from another, a few simple farms. As engaging as this rural vision is, it takes in only a part of the real landscape of turn-of-century southern Massachusetts, for at the mouths of those harbors and the roots of those peninsulas lay noisy, smoky, and rapidly expanding towns and cities. The largest city was New Bedford, where Howland's family had been leading citizens since early colonial days, and which, well before Llewellyn's birth in 1877, had become the home of an increasing number of great textile factories that had caused the region's center of economic gravity to shift from the sea to the shore. *Sou'West and By West of Cape Cod* contains nothing that even hints at the new age: factories are not mentioned, and the only role a city plays is as a place from which to escape, either physically (as in Llewellyn's flight from Boston that opens Chapter Eight) or in the imagination (as in an ancestor's long letter describing the aftermath of the Battle of Trafalgar, which takes up most of Chapter Three). If any community plays an important role in these stories, it is the yachting center near New Bedford that is officially called Dartmouth or South Dartmouth, but which is popularly known by the name of Padanaram, after the place that harbored the Biblical Jacob fleeing from family problems.

More than geography is idealized in this book. In his fore-word, Howland hinted as much when he used the word "tales" to describe the contents. This may disappoint readers who want to be assured of the flesh and blood reality of such vivid characters as the Skipper, Aunt Lee, Cap'n Wasque, and Sim, the fisherman of Noman's Land. Nonetheless, the events and people he described were as invented as the geography on which they occurred and lived was romanticized. There was no Skipper and there was no Cottage, and if Llewellyn Howland walked a Middle Road, it was the imagination's path down which this unhappy man fled, like Jacob, seeking hospice in a strange land.

To understand this book, we must learn something of its author's life, for details of which I am grateful to his son Waldo Howland, the founder of the distinguished Concordia boat yard in Padanaram, to his grandson Llewellyn Howland III, and to an essay in the March 1982 issue of *The New England Quarterly* by Dr. Thomas A. McMullin.

The first Howlands arrived in America in the early seventeenth century and soon settled around present-day New Bedford, where they came to prosper in the grand old model of the Quaker merchant, balancing profits and social conciousness. In one trip in 1865, a ship owned by Llewellyn's grandfather, Matthew Howland, brought home half a million dollars worth of whale oil; five years later, he donated an interdenominational chapel to be built in a poor part of the city. In 1871, seven Howland ships were smashed to splinters when the New Bedford whaling fleet was trapped in the ice flows of the Bering Sea, and a few years later four more vessels in the family fleet were lost. The whaling industry was dying anyway, and following the lead of many New Englanders, the author's father, William D. Howland, entered the cotton textile business.

By 1892, William Howland was running two successful mills in New Bedford. He was best known not for his business successes, which to all appearances were fairly substantial, but for the unusual amount of attention that he paid to his workers' welfare. Propelled by the idealism that he had inherited from his Quaker ancestors, who had been passionate about abolition and the rights of workers and women, he adopted the "New Harmony" social agenda of the British reformer Robert Owen. He had happy relations with unions, paid good wages, and built unusually comfortable, attractive, and low-rent houses for his workers. Unlike other textile companies, he did not reduce weekly wages when the state mandated that the work week be dropped from sixty to fifty-eight hours. In 1894, he refused to go along with a large reduction in wages that textile manufacturers had agreed on when he was out of town; the other mills were struck, but his stayed open. When he had to reduce his work force, he allowed the laid-off workers to live rent-free in company houses. Despite the costs of these benefits, Howland continued to issue dividends through the terrible depression years of the mid-'nineties. But in the spring of 1897, the Howland mills and their utopian world failed, and William Howland died at the age of 44.

Llewellyn Howland was then a freshman at Harvard. He left college to take a job in Boston and eventually became an executive in the construction materials and oil businesses. His passion throughout his life was sailing and cruising in the waters of Buzzards Bay in a succession of sailboats, the last of which was the original of the now-famous Concordia Yawl class of cruising sailboats, which his son Waldo built for him in 1940.

When his wife died in 1939, Howland, who was 61 and

largely retired from business, had trouble adjusting to widowerhood. His son Llewellyn, Jr. suggested that it might help if he were to write down some of the tales with which he had entertained family and friends during evenings afloat and ashore. He worked slowly and painfully; Waldo Howland remembers seeing the study light in his father's house on at two in the morning. Born on those long nights and from wounds gouged in his soul by past adversities and disappointments came these cheerful stories of another New Bedford utopia: a land peopled by gentle folk eager to please and ruled (more successfully than William Howland ever ruled his mills) by the beneficient Skipper, that master of all good knowledge and perpetual friend of lonely boys.

This is a man's world — not in the macho way, but a world of gentle caring and nurturing by men for men. In many of these stories, meals cooked by men are the settings for the cementing or renewing of friendships or for the telling of wonderful tales. Last Fourth of July, I used the chowder recipe that is included in Chapter Two, and the meal was excellent. The last and heartiest of the meals in Sou'West and By West of Cape Cod is the climax of the tale of a thoroughly Dickensian Christmas, told in Chapter Fourteen, and behind it there lay another dream. For a period during World War II, Howland found himself unable to celebrate Christmas, and around then he wrote "Holly Days." The great cheerful meal, with its ritualistic preparations, may be read as a wish, much the way that the Skipper was a wish. I am pleased to report that at least one of Llewellyn Howland's wishes came true, for after he was remarried in 1947, he celebrated joyful Christmases until his death a decade later.

JOHN ROUSMANIERE *has often sailed the waters of Buzzards Bay, the setting of many of these stories. A free-lance writer who lives in Stamford, Connecticut, he is the author of thirteen books on boating, among them* The Golden Pastime: A New History of Yachting, Fastnet, Force 10, *and* The Annapolis Book of Seamanship.

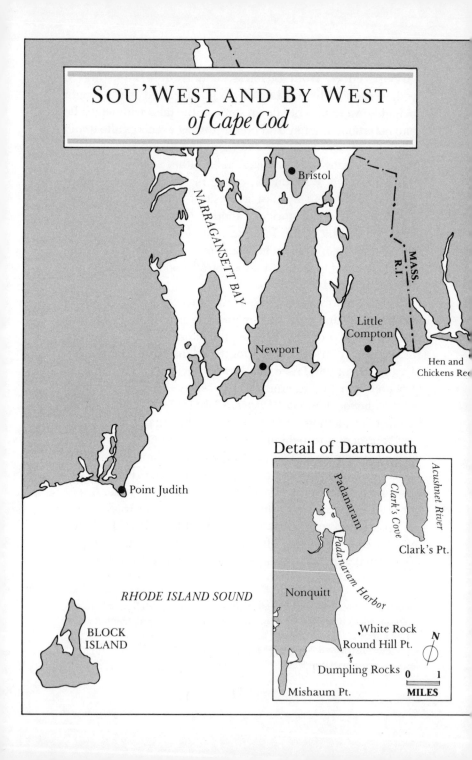

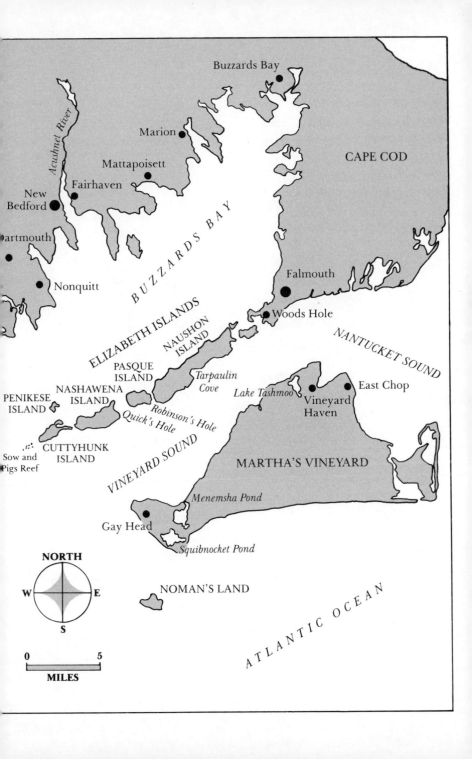

ONE

The Key to the Lighthouse

REVIEWING the long tally of my years, as I do now so often, I am forever finding fresh evidence that I can love, with that fervor which stirs the very clay in my bones, but one small region of all in this wide world. Here in this narrow, sea-bitten strip, stretching from Cape Cod to Point Judith, there is no scenery to awe the spirit or startle the eye. And yet, after long living with this countryside, gentle but still in part untamed, one comes to be deeply stirred when, as so often happens, every feature and outline of it becomes blurred and roundly smoothed by the magic touch of a blue, impalpable haze drifting over it from the ocean.

And, strangely enough, when inwardly I survey this well-loved land — my native sod — I come to it always by way of a road, or rather a country lane.

Planned and built by cattle and farm wagons, this lane meanders along a ridge forming the backbone of Clark's Point, the westerly of two long fingers of land between which the Acushnet River merges with Buzzards Bay. Not only do I see this road and travel it, but I also catch a whiff of sweetness — a mingling of the perfumes breathed out by the creamy white spires on the Clethra bushes, by wild roses, and by the blossoms of wild grapevines with which, when I first came to know it, the lane was flanked.

Always when this picture comes to mind, there, locked into it and making it alive, is the active figure of the Skipper — a cousin, of a degree, and of an older generation — who, with no family of his own and with both means and leisure at his disposal, took me under his wing at the moment when I was ripe and eager to be inducted into that great fellowship of those by whose hands and skill the world's work is carried on.

Little did I realize on that summer morning more than half a century ago, when I was called from home to Grandfather's garden in New Bedford, that the Skipper, who was waiting for me there to give me a silver-mounted watch and a finely braided leather guard, was also about to open a door for me into a new world, rich in treasure beyond price, by inviting me to make him a visit — the first of a long succession that followed through the years as I grew into manhood.

From that day when I first drove over the "Middle Road," as that lane of mine was called, I have felt a deep affection for it, not only because of its sweet-smelling hedgerows, its views of farm lands and pastures and distant glimpses of river and bay; but, of more importance, because after many gentle turns and ups and downs between gray stone walls and weathered buildings, with here and there a stand of trees or a twisted, windshorn single oak, it delivered me at a white-painted gate, the entrance to "The Cottage" — by which name the Skipper's homestead was known.

I have no knowledge of how this farm of two hundred acres or more came to be called The Cottage, for from the first I accepted the name without question, as I accepted the other features. And now, when it would mean so much to me to know why it was so designated and who chose the site and established its beginnings, there is no one left alive of the many who once could have enlightened me.

But, whoever the founder, it was manifest that to him the general lay of the land was of prime importance. He, or she, or, as I like to believe, *they* — a newly married couple — must have spent many happy hours afoot, in all seasons, surveying the countryside and weighing problems of drainage, sites for buildings, exposure to prevailing winds, landscape and seascape, upland, lowland, woodland, and seashore, before coming to the decision to pitch their home on this site. I have even persuaded myself that before undertaking to settle permanently they made trial of this land of their choice by building and living in a temporary house, or cottage, as such a structure would have been called in those days; and that, by the time experience had proved their wisdom, the title "The Cottage" had become so dear to them and so familiar to their neighbors that, inappropriate as it was for such habitation as they finally achieved, it was allowed to stand.

That generously wide, white gate slung between rough, quarried granite posts spoke eloquently of permanence; for, heavily constructed of locust — the timber that outweathers even our New England stone — it was so "backed, bolted, braced an' stayed" against sag that, in spite of its weight, it could be swung open with ease on its great hinges of wrought bog-iron. And I can remember my pride on the day my rating was advanced from mere passenger to member of the farm crew when, on our coming to the halt before this barrier, I was ordered to "shake a leg and tend gate." Not only was this an elevation in rank, but it carried with it a long-desired privilege; for, after the horses and wagon had passed through the opening and continued on their way along the entrance drive of crushed oyster shell, I was free to let go my hold of the gate, jump onto it, and ride it home, as of its own accord it swept through a broad arc with the sensation of an elemental force, presently to close with a ponderous clank as the long iron latch dropped precisely into the striker.

17

Here, aloft on an upper bar, I could look eastward across the Middle Road and the half mile of gently sloping fields fenced with gray stone that lay between me and the shores of the Acushnet estuary. I could see a little beach of white sand and the building sheds and marine railway of Beetle's Boat Yard sprawling on its margin and, beyond, a sail or two of shipping bearing the commerce of New Bedford. Sight of these sails set my mind roving to distant islands and tropic seas. I dreamed dreams of a day when perhaps I should be taking part in faraway ventures.

As I clung there on my perch, idling with thoughts of the future, I was recalled to the present by a dog's low whine, and looking down I saw Prince, a tawny collie, the faithful watchman of the farm. He had the well-known expression of eye and cock to his long nose that conveyed rebuke. I felt I had been caught slacking. I jumped to the ground to follow him as he trotted along a footpath which, branching from the white driveway, led westward across the "East Mowing," close along its north bound — shortly to cut through a stand of white oak and beech.

As Prince and I were passing through this thin belt of woodland — a screen against cold, northeasterly weather and the public highway — I can remember a sensation of well-being sweeping over me. It seemed as if I were crossing a threshold into a smiling world, from which all doubt and disorder had been banished, where I had a clear-cut, useful role to play; and, as we emerged from the shade of the trees and came to a little gate in a fence, my feeling that all here was well deepened to thorough contentment.

We stopped for a minute to peer through the pickets into the "Peach Alley" — a long, narrow, half acre of tillage with a strip of lawn down the center. Sheltered from the north by a row of spiring Norway spruce and bounded east and west by ten-foot, flat-topped stone walls, the alley formed an ingenious catchall for the sun. Within ten feet or so of the walls were ranged two regiments of carefully pruned peach trees — mature bearers alternating with saplings — a late-fruiting, yellow freestone variety to the west and an earlier strain, also yellow, to the east. A peach's heart had to be cold and its nature sour indeed not to be stirred and sweetened by the warmth of stored sunshine released from those stone walls on gray days and chilly nights, as advancing summer deepened the flush on the ripening fruit!

Beyond the alley our path merged with the white drive, which, still heading west, ran between a spiky hedge of hawthorn and a long rank of farm buildings and sheds. Halfway along the rank the hedge ended, to allow the drive to make a right-angle turn to the south and shortly lose itself in a courtyard paved with brick. At the far end of this pavement the shell drive came to life again to curve sharply west around a clump of primeval beech trees and twist its way down a quarter mile of steeply sloping fields to the "West Gate," which opened on a right of way giving access to the sandy beaches and shingly foreshores of Clark's Cove.

Here at the end of the hedge, within sight of home, Prince turned about and trotted off on another errand. Released from the urge of his shepherding, I surrendered to "that Spring feeling" of this afternoon in early June and sat down on a whitewashed boulder marking the turn of the drive. On my left ran the pink glory of the hedge in blossom, alive and faintly humming with myriad bees. Ahead stretched the paved court, flanked on the east by five gnarled old buttonwoods and the well house, and on the west by the long pile of the farmhouse itself. I watched the cool shadow of this building creep over the strip of lawn at its base, to widen gradually until it was halfway across the mossy brick pavement. I saw the many panes of the long windows turn blank as the light of the eastern sky faded. I saw the brilliance die out of the yellow and green lichens splotching the rough granite of the house walls where they showed between shaggy masses of English ivy that clung to them. I watched Isabelle, the sleek catbird, slip into her nest among the ivy leaves; I heard the serenade of her mate as he balanced on a nearby frond. I felt I might be caught up, in another moment, to drift away on the wisp of blue smoke from the kitchen chimney . . . when suddenly I was startled wide awake by the click of an opening door, from which came Deborah, the cook and general manager within-doors. Aware that she, like Prince, was intolerant of idling, I sprang from my seat and ran to meet her at the well.

This "house well," as it was called, was in reality a spring that seeped up through a deep seam in the granite outcrop on the various levels of which the house, courtyard, "South Terrace," and sunk garden, with its three dark, tower-like Irish yews, were founded. The reservoir for the cold, clear water was a roughly circular excavation some eight feet across by twenty deep, quarried out of the ledge and capped with thick slabs of North River bluestone. Dogged to the capping was the well house — a rectangle twelve feet by fifteen, heavily timbered, and with a roof the shape of the tester over a four-posted bed. On three of the sides were louvered panels for ventilation; on the fourth, toward the house, a door with a window.

"Well, Mister Lazy Bones! I told the folks you'd be on hand when supper time came," said Deb, as I joined her in the dim coolness of the well house. Darting a glance at her right hand, I was relieved to see she was not armed with the large brass thimble that so often flicked my ear when I came within reach — so, ignoring the reproachful greeting, I leaned against the breast-high well curb beside her to peer down the ferny shaft and help her lower the heavy, oak-staved bucket. As it ran smoothly down, the counterweight — a triple-shelved cage — came up on the other end of the rope that rendered over a big lignum-vitae pulley suspended from the coved roof above. On the shelves of the cage were ranged crocks, pitchers, bowls of butter, eggs, cheese, cream, and, in their seasons, lettuce, asparagus, tomatoes, plums, peaches, strawberries, and grapes — for it was Debby's belief that these and other products of the

20

farm were of so delicate a nature that chilling in the well shaft "done 'em good," while icing "done 'em harm."

Having charged a copper-lined tray with articles from the shelves, Debby lowered the cage, to hoist the now full bucket until it was tripped on the metal lip of a small wooden trough with a spout projecting through the curbing, which flumed the crystal water into a dark red pitcher of porous Fayal pottery that stood below on the stone capping. With the tray and pitcher between us we crossed the courtyard into the kitchen.

Here was the very heart of the house — a big square room with both east and west windows and a chimney breast occupying the entire north wall, with a cast-iron range in the middle flanked by the brick oven and an archway into the summer kitchen and offices beyond. Half the floor was of silverstone flagging, to withstand the wear and tear between range and long sink with its polished copper hand pump and a deal dresser opposite, along the east wall. The other half of the floor was of wide pine planks, painted black and peppered with fine spatters of white, with a final coat of yellow varnish making of it a dark-green mirror to reflect the legs of chairs and the one big central table of bird's-eye maple. Overhead, the plaster of the ceiling, cream-tinted by age, was broken into panels by oak beams, their time-darkened faces slightly rippled from strokes of the adze with which they had been hewn, and from which, on big hooks, hung burlapped hams, bacon, ropes of onions, and baskets of all sizes and shapes. The walls were sheathed from floor to ceiling with native pine, which the passing years had toned to old ivory. Always there hung about this room the savor, cleanly but pungent, of good living. I could have dawdled here with pleasure but for Debby's brisk industry, which drove me on into the pantry, from which the way led up three stone steps into the dining room. Through a door opening into the "gun room" streamed the late afternoon light, inviting me to enter; and there, as I had hoped, I found the Skipper.

Sitting close under a window that looked out over the sharp-ly pitched "West Mowing" to Clark's Cove, he was tying a new snapper on a riding whip. As he bent over his task the level rays of the evening sun accentuated the ruddiness of his face and glinted through the grizzling brown hair and moustache. His muscular hands were very deft in all their movements. Without looking up, he said:

"Well, old man, what about a moonlight ride after supper? That 'Dicky' of yours is just pining for work . . . Run upstairs and have a look at what's waiting for you on your bed."

The main staircase at The Cottage was an ingenious contri-vance — an integral part of the great central chimney stack, with three right-angle turns in its short course. Its start was in a small entry, opposite the front door with its two upper panels of glass bull's-eyes. The second-story landing was directly above the entry below. Two of the bedrooms opened onto this land-ing. To reach the other rooms one had to pass through the bedroom to the left. This stair arrangement, while a great saver of space, had drawbacks, and there came a time when I had to surmise that the bedsteads, bureaus, and tallboys must have been built where they stood in those upper rooms — while Debby gave point to her disapproval of the "contraption" by saying: "It ain't decent to die where you and your coffin's got to be lowered out a winder on a rope's end." Nevertheless I liked those stairs, for they lifted and dropped you quickly. There was nothing tedious about them; and on that particular evening they chimed with my eagerness to get to my room.

There on the bed lay a pair of brown whipcord riding breeches, lower-leg buttons, leather knee patches, and all — a possession long desired that would boost me one more rung up the ladder to man's estate. The minute I had them on and started downstairs again I realized they gave me the wide-kneed, bow-legged action I so coveted. I think the Skipper was repaid for the trouble he'd taken over this detail of my equipment as, in my best horsy manner, I rejoined him to stammer my thanks.

On summer evenings such as this, when the Skipper and I were alone, we had our suppers in the gun room, where the glow of the western sky gave us ample light. On this occasion Debby appeared without warning, and after relentlessly sweeping off the "litter," as she called whatever she found on the very battered table used as both workbench and desk, she served us a planked Taunton River shad and a cold platter of young asparagus and hollandaise sauce. The stalks, all green and only about three inches long, were tenderly edible from tip to butt. Deb followed this delectable combination with a home-made cream cheese, toasted rye crusts, and breakfast cups of black coffee, "so's to keep from fallin' asleep in the saddle."

The moon was high enough when we started our ride that night to transform the familiar Middle Road into a mysterious way of black and silver patches. Both "Dicky" and the Skipper's Kentucky horse, "Oscar Wilde" — so named because of occasional lapses from grace — shied and snorted as they faced the shifting tree shadows. I blessed my new breeches, which helped me to keep reasonable contact with my saddle — a feat which, to my shame, was then and always has been difficult.

The object of our expedition was the delivery of a letter to the keeper of the lighthouse atop the fort that occupied the tip end of Clark's Point. This fort, a project of the Civil War, had never been entirely completed. Unmounted cannon and piles of stone and brick lay about the approach to the central gate. We had our work cut out to get our horses through and around this raffle, which took on weird shapes in the deceptive moon-light. Dismounting at the entrance, the Skipper, who was to stop below with Dicky and Oscar, gave me the letter and pointed out the niche where the big brass key of the wicket gate was kept. Past this barrier, I came into a cavernous darkness where my footfalls on granite floors echoed and where infre-quent shafts of light from the open gun ports gave me my bearings. I groped my way through long corridors and vaulted casemates. I climbed many flights of stone stairs, finally to step out on the roof, which was protected by steeply sloping turfed earthworks. Tucked away between two of these embankments was a little white door, beyond which twisted a corkscrew iron stairway leading to the lantern room of the lighthouse.

After handing over the letter I was invited to "sit a spell," to watch the keeper tend the multiple lamp. As aboard the flagship of a fleet, "spit and polish" was the keynote here in Uncle Sam's aerie. This first visit at night to a lighthouse gave me an abiding confidence in these "aids to navigation," and as I retraced my steps I was almost persuaded that government service was the life I'd choose to follow.

For our way home to The Cottage we chose the grassy, unshadowed path along the shore of Clark's Cove, where we could let the horses run. The cool air whistling in our ears and the slight clinking of the bits made a pleasant music. When we came to our own West Gate we pulled down to a walk, and, turning off the track, crossed a sandy beach where Oscar and Dicky, wading in shallow water, could cool their legs. The moon, now well aloft, threw a broad path of flickering radiance across the little waves of the Cove. The gentle northwest land breeze stirred the new leaves of three giant tupelos that marked the landward margin of the beach. Spellbound and silent, we sat there for a while until the Skipper said:

"I wouldn't call Joshua a fool if he'd tried, on a night like this, to stay the moon in her course. It makes me fairly ache to think I can't halt it all, to be looked at as long as ever we want to — but I know something of it will stick by you to the end." And, with a sigh, he turned Oscar shoreward.

At a slow walk, with loose rein and creaking leather, we came up the steep drive to the front door of The Cottage, where the Skipper, swinging out of the saddle, left me to stable the horses — a gratifying proof of confidence. Later, as I crept up that narrow, tortuous stairway I heard the soft-toned bell of the grandfather clock in the dining room strike twelve.

Yes, the Skipper was right! For the memories of that night and many, many other nights and days centering about The Cottage — a truly golden age — have stuck by me. And it has been brought home to me how blessed I was to have such a friend, companion, and mentor as the Skipper during that period when I was neither boy nor man.

With him as my leader and The Cottage as training ground, my visits, which were timed with my vacations from school and college, gradually came to be filled with the business of education, in the truest sense of that word. For nowhere and no-when has there been contrived an institution of learning more richly endowed or more fruitful in results than this New England shore farm. Here I learned to swim; to sail a boat; to dig clams and catch fish and clean and cook 'em; to respect and deal with a cow's tail at milking time; to feed and tend horses, pigs, and poultry; to be on deferential terms with bees; to work with tools and know ash from oak; and, of more consequence than these arts and many others, to feel I was doing my part in a vitally important work, along with King, the farmer; Willie and Levi, the farm boys; Prince, the watchdog; and Tim and Tip, the terriers; Deborah in the kitchen; and — above all others — the Skipper.

Is it so strange, when inwardly surveying this land so dear to me, that I should always enter it by way of the Middle Road, that Highway to Happiness — a happiness so enduring yet so simple, which has stirred the desire to in some part share it with others?

TWO

Menemsha

D EBORAH, the cook, had "stepped out to see her folks"
that afternoon of a late September day, leaving the
Skipper and me for a time masters of The Cottage and
free to choose and provide our supper, and, what was more, eat
it where and when we felt inclined.

It was too late in the day to go fishing, and yet, with the blue
glinting water of the Cove lapping gently on the shingle at the
foot of the lawn, a craving for spoils of the sea was so compelling that shortly we were searching the low-tide shallows for
Bay scallops.

The Skipper was equipped with waders and a long-handled
dip net, while I had on my thigh gum boots and towed a gunny
sack. By keeping our backs toward the westering sun, and with
the gentle breeze from the same quarter, we had good vision
through the two or three feet of clear water that covered the
eelgrass and patches of sand where the quarry lay — sometimes in numerous colonies and again in ones and twos. Working from north to south in order that the northeasterly trending

wavelets might carry the rile of our footsteps away from us, the Skipper, without overextending himself, was able to dip up in the course of an hour or so three quarters of a bushel of selected "fish," which, after every fruitful scoop, I would retrieve from his net and stow in my sack.

We'd brought our simple gear to high-water mark in a wheelbarrow — not one of the wooden horrors of mass production, but one so designed and built that, with its big, broad-tired wheel, its light but strong frame, and its balance when loaded with our dripping plunder, gave to one trundling it up to The Cottage a feeling of power and ease rather than of disagreeable labor.

Before shucking our scallops that evening we divided the lot by count. When each of us had his half piled at his left on the long wooden bench in the scullery and our knives in hand ready for business, the Skipper said, "Go!" and the plump, creamy "eyes" began to plop swiftly into two glazed earthenware bowls at our right. This making a race of it was to settle a long-disputed question of technique. It was also an endurance test, for when the Skipper won by a half dozen or so I was wondering whether or not I could last the course, and ached all over from nervous tension.

By tacit agreement, as the Skipper picked up the two bowls and left me alone in the scullery, I understood that every trace of our operations there must be scrubbed and scalded away before Deborah should return. My final act of cleaning up was another trip to the beach, where the damning evidence of shells and offal could be disposed of safely below high-water mark.

As I pushed the barrow up the path again toward the house in the now cool darkness, I could see by a wavering rosy reflection on the panes of one of the long windows that the Skipper had a fire alight on the hearth in the gun room, and a tide of satisfaction seemed to well up around me as I sensed the snugness of that retreat for "menfolks."

This feeling of well-being was in no way dulled as I came into the room, where I found the Skipper before an old battered pine table, very busy with a rolling pin and cutting board, reducing bread crusts to an aggregate of crisp brown crumbs. On the hearth, toasting themselves in the bland heat of a deep bed of glowing embers, were an old-fashioned tin kitchen and two oak kegstaves, on edge, flanking it. These staves had been buttered and then plastered on their concave faces with a half-inch mortar of well-scalded and salted Rhode Island gray cornmeal.

Setting aside his rolling pin, the Skipper brushed the crumbs into a loose pile on the board and turned to a platter on which were ranged perhaps three dozen of the scallop eyes. Picking these up one by one, he gave each a dip in a saucer of olive oil, a roll in the crumbs, and passed them to me to be threaded on a long skewer. When the last scallop had been spitted we locked the skewer and its brown beads into the tin kitchen.

As I sat down on an old milking stool, prepared to turn the handle of the spit, the Skipper warned me. "Don't play 'Yankee Doodle' on that tonight. 'Dead March' from *Saul* is about the right timing." So, reining my hungry impatience, I sat there cranking slowly while the Skipper disappeared, to return shortly with a tray on which was half a Ponderosa lemon, a roll of butter, Austrian paprika, a jug of new cider, a dusty bottle of port, a green glazed jar of African dates preserved in pink syrup, and the requisite silverware, glass, and crockery.

By the time these things had been set out on the table and the two fat spermaceti candles that gave us our light had been freshened with the snuffer, the scallops were showing signs of having had as much toasting as they could bear, and the ashcakes on the staves were a golden brown.

Every mouthful of that supper "done us good" — particularly the sweet, tender scallops with a drop of lemon juice and pinch of paprika on them; so that, when at last we turned away from the table to face the fire that now, replenished with

28

hickory and apple-wood fagots, was shooting tongues of yellow flame up the devouring throat of the fireplace, I felt that realization had, for once, equaled anticipation.

While the Skipper sipped his port and crunched the last of his ashcake it dawned on me that, so long as I had known a scallop, I had accepted the fact that the part of him we ate was called an "eye," while at the same time I was fully aware that this delicious morsel was in no way connected with his vision, but was in reality the muscle by which this extremely lively bivalve could on occasion clap his shells like castanets. "Why is this so?" I wondered, and forthwith asked the "Old Man."

Before answering, he took his time to light one of his Manila cheroots and savor the first long and fragrant pull on it; and then at last, with a look that passed me by and seemed to bore deep into gone years, he spun this yarn:

"It must be nearly half a century since I asked my grandfather the very question you've asked me. It was an early December day in the old gray house — the farthest out on the Point here. We'd had a mess of scallops for midday dinner and had just finished the last of them when I asked for information. The old gentleman did not answer; but instead bundled himself into his winter cap, comforter, and heavy overcoat; and after helping me into similar warm wraps he drove me ahead of him up the attic ladder through the roof trap and out onto the captain's walk that stretched along the ridgepole between the two big chimneys. From this vantage point we could sweep Buzzards Bay from Woods Hole to Cuttyhunk with the long spyglass that was kept on a rack between two rafters, handy to the scuttle.

"The weather was clear — moderate northerly — the best sort for picking up the private signal flying at the main truck of a homeward-bound ship that had reached into Vineyard Sound and anchored in Tarpaulin Cove. There she would wait for a southerly slant of wind which would allow her to fetch through Quick's Hole, cross the Bay, and finally run up the Acushnet River into New Bedford harbor.

"Because she was lying head on to us, it was difficult for Grandfather to make certain of the ship's flag; but after several minutes' peering he gave a sigh of satisfaction, lowered the glass, slapped its joints together, and said:

" 'Run down and tell thy grandmother that the *Ann Alexander* is in Tarpaulin Cove and that thee and I will be starting in the *Panther* within an hour to visit Captain Snow and get the news of his voyage. Thee can help her stow the grub in the hamper while I keep on the heels of Gumbo and Jahazael and get the mainsail hoisted and the jib loosed.'

"The *Panther* was a fifty-foot sloop Grandfather kept moored in a little bight on the east side of the Point for such expeditions as this of ours and an occasional fishing trip. She belied her name, being neither lithe nor lean. Instead she had tremendous beam, apple-cheeked bows, and a fine run — a regular cod-head and mackerel-tail model — and, with the center-board hoisted, a shoal draft. To windward she was an indifferent performer, but on a reach or a run, fast and comfortable. If anyone twitted him on the *Panther*'s inability to sail close-hauled, Grandfather would explain that, as a retired seafarer, at his age he had earned the right to keep the wind eternally on his back instead of his face and that he was through forever with 'shovin' and pushin' ' to windward. I found he even went a step farther as to the wind, for on that chilly December afternoon, as the *Panther* ran swiftly across the Bay toward Robinson's Hole, the old gentleman went below directly we had dropped the mooring, to toast his face in the pleasant warmth of the big cook stove and euchre the wind entirely.

"It was dark when we anchored deep in Tarpaulin Cove that late afternoon, and I can remember how, by the time we had the sails furled, Jupiter, Mars, and Sirius were firing the placid water around us. It was a night in a thousand — cold and so crystal clear the stars seemed to snap as they winked. It gave me a cable-laid twist, so that by the time Gumbo, the colored boy, had the cold corned beef, cottage-fried potatoes, apple turnovers, and coffee on the table, I had to sit on my hands to keep from snatching while Grandfather asked a silent blessing.

"Before I felt I had more than commenced my supper I noticed Grandfather was shuffling his feet — a sure sign that a squall of impatience was building up. I knew this was unhealthy weather to be caught out in, and so I quickly lined up my knife and fork on my plate and looked as satisfied as I could. It must have been a good try on, for by the time we were in the dory, with Jahazael at the oars, headed for the *Ann Alexander,* Grandfather was reminiscing about the Cove in Revolutionary days — a sure sign that the squall had blown by.

"As we came alongside that little ship (she was only eighty-nine feet long) the tale of her wanderings could almost be read by the varied odors wafted out from her. There were the coconuts of the Pacific atolls, the mildews of Cape Horn, the cockroaches of Brazil, all tangled and held together by the sweetish, sickly smell of sperm oil in oak casks.

"Having hailed her, we climbed aboard at the starboard mizzen chain plates, while Captain Snow gave us a hand as we went over the rail and dropped on deck. He and Grandfather immediately went below to the cabin, as I knew they would, to talk, talk, talk about such uninteresting things as the price of oil and candles. Jahazael could not and I would not follow them to that region of knives and forks in the stern. Instead, after the painter of the dory was fast, he and I made a beeline forward to the fore-castle, where I knew there would be a treasure house of curios and scrimshaw work to look at and plenty of tall yarns to hear.

"What an evening it was! But again I was not half satisfied, when I heard a familiar voice coming from on deck at the head of the ladder, saying:

" 'What is thee doing down there? Doesn't thee know it's long after bedtime? Come! Shake a leg or Gumbo'll have fallen asleep and let the fire go out and we'll shiver all night.'

"On the way over to the *Panther* I asked if it had been a good voyage.

" 'She's bung full and Captain Snow says he's even filled all the old boots. Thee can see she's pretty low in the water.'

"This was good news for me, too. I felt Grandfather would be, so to speak, malleable; so I tried him again with:

" 'Thee hasn't told me yet why what we eat of a scallop is called an eye.'

" 'And I'm not going to now, my boy. But if it's fair tomorrow we'll run over to Menemsha and let Monohansett Joe satisfy thy curiosity.'

"We started the next day early and were well across Vineyard Sound before the sun rose with promise of another fine day. Jahazael set us ashore in the dory on the beach of Menemsha Bight, well to the westward of Gay Head, and from there we watched him until he had reboarded the *Panther* and had her on her course up the Sound toward Holmes Hole (now Vineyard Haven), where he was to anchor and wait for us to come overland by horse and wagon.

"To reach Joe's little farm we had to cover about three miles of uneven, rolling moorland that, sloping gently to the eastward, skirted the great tidal salt lake known as Menemsha Pond. For most of the distance, we could follow some one of the innumerable sheep paths that led all whither through dun-colored winter grass and leafless clumps of bayberry. At almost every step, up would soar a meadowlark, to sail downwind away from us, leaving behind a train of plaintive, fairy-like music. We seemed bewitched, and I, for one, felt I had come to a new world by the time we reached the weatherbeaten, lichened cabin on the very margin of an arm of the Pond, where this handsome old Gay Head Indian friend of ours lived.

"We found him splitting driftwood on the lee side of the building, and Grandfather said to him:

" 'Joe, we've come over from Tarpaulin, where Captain Snow's lying in the *Ann Alexander* waiting for a slant to run into Bedford, and we want thee to make us a chowder and then drive us over to Holmes Hole. Does thee think thee can accommodate us?'

" 'Reckon I can,' said Joe, 'if thee'll give us time. My horse and me's gettin' stiff in the joints for cold-weather travelin'.'

"Looking out across the sheltered pool at our feet where Joe moored his dory and a couple of skiffs, I noticed the calm, glassy surface was constantly broken by little dark splashes. There were so many of these breaks and they came so constantly that there was a patter like rain. I was puzzled and must have shown it, for I came out of a trance to hear Joe say:

" 'Has thee never seen first-year scallops gettin' ready to move into deep water before the ice comes? Them youngsters are comin' up now to have a look at the weather. They'll all be moved out come evenin'. Thee'll be froze out, too, if thee don't come inside where thy gran'dad's been settin' by the fire for some spell.'

"Inside, that little house was shipshape — the neatest, cleanest you ever saw. In the one big room Joe had his workshop — tools, bench, and all; there was all his gear for fishing, eeling, clamming, and fowling; his cook stove, blacked and shining like Grandfather's Sunday boots; the sink and polished copper pump; a ship's built-in bunk; a table that folded against the wall; light but comfortable chairs of his own make; but not a 'boughten' useless gimcrack in the place — even the air there smelled useful.

"With a good fire going in the stove, Joe set about preparing the chowder. He was so skillful that Grandfather and I just sat and watched. From the bucket of soft-shelled clams that he brought in from the woodshed (he was careful to explain that they had neither been drowned nor frozen), he selected about forty-five small ones and put them aside in a wooden bowl. Six small white onions were then cut into thin rings and fed slowly, one at a time, into a saucepan of already boiling water. While the onions were seething furiously on the hottest lid of the stove, he peeled six medium-sized potatoes, sliced them thin,

33

and set them to boiling with two quarts of milk in a double boiler. By the time he had the potatoes and milk going strong, he moved the onions onto the back of the stove and put a big heavy-lidded kettle, an eighth full of salt water, in their place. When this salt water had begun to steam and jiggle the lid, the clams, shells and all, were dumped in and the lid clapped on again. After the potatoes and milk had been cooking for twenty minutes or so, Joe slowly mixed in with them a white sauce — pretty thick — seasoned with not too much salt and a good dose of black pepper, and set the whole to cook again. He now took the big kettle over to the sink, scooped out the clams with a long-handled skimmer, shucked them, and, cutting off the black tips of the snouts, chopped the balance fine in a wooden tray and then poured them in with the milk and potatoes, adding two cupfuls of the 'clam liquor' from the kettle, and all the onion rings. The chowder was now allowed to boil two minutes more and then, piping hot, was set on the table in the double boiler and ladled into deep earthenware bowls. A plate of hard ship's bread (hardtack) was the side dish for our chowder and hand-wrought iron spoons that must have been very old, the conveyors.

"After we were well into our second bowl Grandfather said: 'Joe, I can feel every spoonful of thy chowder makin' Kyle the instant it reaches bottom.'

"Joe looked pleased, but I wondered if, like all the rest of our friends and family, he was hazy as to the nature of this elixir 'Kyle,' that Grandfather seemed to generate whenever his palate was pleased. Without expecting an answer the old gentleman continued:

" 'This boy of mine's been pestering me for the last two days to tell him how scallop meats came to be called 'eyes' — and I told him thee was the only man in the world that knew and had a right to tell the secret. It will please me if thee'll tell the whole story.'

"At this Joe's rather severe face lightened up, and turning toward me he said:

" 'My folks were born, lived, and died on the Vineyard here for long — years and years before thy folks come in their ships. I was born over across the Sound on Monohansett [Little Island], in Lackey's Bay. My mother and father were on a summer fishing in their canoe. That's how I get my name. My grandfather told me about the scallop eyes when I was a boy like thee. His grandfather told him. All grandfathers in my family tell grandsons of times so far back that Vineyard and Noman's all one island. In them days scallops were no account — hadn't good sweet eyes, just watery bellies; lay on the bottom like oysters — never come up like we see 'em out there today.

" 'One year, at dusk, hell of big canoe with one mast an' big red an' white sail come pokin' into Bight. Tide was slack, water high, an' her crew run her up the canal into the Pond, ten or twelve oars a-side, double-banked. They beached her before they seen any o' us. Our folks lay under cover an' watched 'em. That night they had a big fire on shore an' after eatin' their vittles they lay round the fire to sleep, with watchers takin' turns to keep the fire goin'. In the mornin' my grandfather of them days, first mate to Gay Head Indian Captain, went down to palaver with these strange folks. When he come back he says they were all pink an' white with hair like light corn silk. They were all men but one. *She* was boss, an' very tall an' good-lookin'. They cut down trees an' made houses, they come fishin' with us folks, they eat clams an' oysters an' stayed all winter, cuttin' oak knees an' crotches. They were friendly an' good boatmen. Our folks made out they come from long ways to eastward.

" 'The woman was a great hand for walkin' 'round the shores of the Pond watchin' the shore birds an' singin' to herself, an' one early afternoon before those folks set out for home, this boss woman came round on this side of the Pond

35

lookin' across toward the high land yonder. By damn! If all the scallops in that Pond didn't begin to rise an' break water. After that, every time that woman went walkin' near the Pond them scallops would rise, an' they kep' this up until the ice came to hold 'em down under. So then my folks knew scallops had grown eyes a-purpose to rise an' have a look at this stranger, an' they took some ashore an' watched 'em, an' see they opened an' shut their shells quick as a wink an' peeked out when they thought nobody was lookin'.

" 'Then they shucked some, an' there, sure enough, were them white, creamy eyes, that's good eatin' when you get used to 'em. An' ever since them days,' said Joe, 'at this time o' year thee'll see them scallops risin' an' risin' in hopes they'll catch sight o' that handsome woman again.' "

THREE

Trafalgar

I WAS emotionally a little above myself, for it was the day I had graduated from kilt skirts to trousers, when I first made acquaintance with melgers. These delectable sweetmeats, which I believe were a compound of molasses, caramel, chopped beechnuts, and snowy icing, lay hidden in the belly of a big glazed jar of deep blue, shot with cherry blossoms. The jar — after that introduction an irresistible siren — was confined in a locked closet in a quiet old mansion house not a stone's throw from that of my grandfather in New Bedford.

Far from the waterfront and business center of the port, these two houses stood screened from other, neighboring rooftrees by the interlacing branches of the great American elms that bordered the streets of this region. Lofty tunnels of cool, green shade in summer, gray Gothic cloisters in winter, these streets were graceful at all times and gave a dignity and charm to the buildings and gardens they served. Here none of the paneled front doors was ever locked, so that it became an almost daily habit of mine to slip through the chalky white one where Grandfather's seafaring treasures lay, or the dark green one where, if Fate were kind, a melger might be the reward of venture.

A turn of the heavy cut-glass doorknob, and the green door could be swung open on well-oiled, noiseless hinges, revealing a long narrow entry stretching to a half-open door on the left, through which streamed light enough to discover a straight, uncompromising staircase with its mahogany handrail dully polished by time's touch and a tall grandfather clock whose steady beat gave life to the otherwise dim silence.

Here by unbreakable lore one paused and gave the password: two low notes, whistled. If an answering whistle came from the room beyond the half-opened door, a glow of pleasure speeded the pulse and set the feet racing across the dull bronze carpet and the threshold into the room of many enchantments where Aunt Lee, the frail mistress of this household, held her court. If the whistle was not answered, the visitor stole sadly out into the prosaic world.

A cold October day with a blustering northwest wind, and the thought of the savor of melgers brought on a sudden desire to lie snug behind the green door. Luck was with me that afternoon, for my whistle was answered, permitting me to enter my "chamber of delights," where the fitful afternoon sun streaming in through west windows brightened the leather bindings of the books on their shelves covering one entire wall and warmed the faded carpet to a glow. A fire of maple logs smouldered in the gray, marble-faced fireplace, and a breath of heliotrope from the glazed plant-room that opened to the south hallowed all with its incense. But, as always, it was my aunt's welcoming smile and her gentle kiss that kindled the feeling of changeless security and faith that enfolded me in this sanctuary.

Born of the moment, some impulse urged me to ask if I might roll a big terrestrial globe, on its casters, from its place under a tallboy to the hearth rug, where I could lie at ease with a reading glass and by a touch revolve and cant the world to any plane or angle suiting my fancy. Presently I was prone at Aunt Lee's feet, sailing swiftly across oceans and striding over continents. Suddenly, through the glass, two crossed swords and "Cape Trafalgar" wheeled into sight to arrest my voyaging. What was the significance of the crossed swords under a name that rolled so pleasantly over my tongue? I pondered for a moment, for I knew idle questions were not encouraged in this room. Then I chanced it:

"Aunt Lee, what *do* crossed swords mean?"

"Places where great battles have been fought," came the answer, and, "Which one are you looking at?"

"Trafalgar — but I thought that was a city square in London. And here it is in Spain."

A silence followed — so long that I turned away from the globe to look at my hostess. She was gazing at me, yet through me, her thoughts evidently far away. At last her eyes came back from their distant quest; she patted the vacant end of the sofa beside her and invited me to "come and sit close."

When I was perched on the deep seat with my legs straight out before me, she said: "You know, it's a strange happening that you should have picked out Trafalgar to ask about today — for it's exactly eighty-two years ago this afternoon, and just off that Cape you were looking at, that Lord Nelson, in command of a fleet of English ships, met and defeated the combined armada of French and Spanish men-of-war that Napoleon — 'Boney' — had sent against him. One of our own ships from New Bedford, the *Ann Alexander,* played a small part in this battle. I'll read you an old, old letter all about it."

Going to the tallboy, she presently came back with a packet of papers. Drawing a low table in front of us, she sat down again beside me, loosed the faded ribbons holding the packet together, and after a moment's search spread out several square sheets giving way at their creases and closely covered with crabbed writing, the ink browned by age. And here is the story as she read it to me fifty-five years ago:

On board ship Ann Alexander
Leghorn. 11/5/1805

My Dear Wife:

As thee will see when thee receives these presents I am still here in this ancient port. I am in good health under Divine Providence and trust this finds thee in like case. On my first arrival the events and perils of the voyage were of such recent occurrence, and I was in such haste to advise thee and George Howland [the owner of the *Ann Alexander*] of our safe arrival, that my mind was jumbled and I could only touch on the exceptional happenings.

But the passing of the days has ordered my thoughts and made clear how mercifully our affairs have prospered by the help of our Heavenly Father, and I want that thee should share my deep gratitude and comprehend the character of one of the episodes of this voyage wherein we encountered without injury to our lives or property an outburst of the evil passions of mankind in a manifestation so terrible to witness even in small part as we did. So I will attempt to describe this collision of great fleets of ships in battle where the mastery of the seas was at hazard.

Thee must understand that *early* on twenty-first day ult. after a week of overcast weather, when having run our distance I was uneasy as to our position and hoping to raise the land about the Straits [Gibraltar], many sails to leeward of us were reported from aloft. The wind was light at northwest, and while I was fearful of falling afoul of French or Spanish letters of marque or worse with the weather what it was, I held our course (a little south of east) in hopes that I might raise a landfall. The strange sails were headed south when first sighted and shortly faded away.

With paltry airs during early forenoon our way was very moderate. By five bells, from fore-topgallant yard where I went with my glass in hopes to pick up land, I discovered a great press of sails to the eastward and more sails to the south, all headed north. With the breeze so light and a heavy and growing swell from SW it was hopeless to come to the wind to beat out of the pocket we were fairly caught in. Accordingly I shortened sail and let her sog to leeward toward what I could now make out to be two squadrons of heavy vessels under a press of sail bearing down obliquely on a raffle of ships beyond.

Thus we proceeded till shortly after noon, when of a sudden a great smoke commenced to billow up from among the ships we were drifting down on, which soon became so thick as to shut them from view, the sluggish wind being too light to lift the pall. As we continued to be hove up and up and then dropped by the great following seas with glassy sides and barrel tops just ruffled by the gentle breeze, it appeared to me we were being drawn by some mysterious magnet into a boiling pot the steam from which was riven here and there by darting tongues of flame, while across the heaving floor came an ever increasing thunder that finally made the ship quiver so that I realized the heft of the broadsides that were being touched off in that mighty cannonading.

And here, I do assure thee, had the weather been such that I could do so to advantage I would have altered course to edge away from these parts, but as we lay, there was nothing we could do but pray for a change that would allow us to move with speed to one side or the other of the battle that in a half moon about two leagues in length stretched athwart our bows. But here the wind if anything took off so that we were impelled more by the scend of the sea than by the tug of our canvas as we approached more near — ourselves in awed silence except for the creak of our spars and rattle of the reef points on our sails when we were becalmed in the troughs; the thunder of

41

the guns coming up to us in waves, not continuous as thee'd expect.

For a while I began to hope that, what with the smoke and the desperate fierceness of the engagement, we in our little barque might drive by the southern horn of the battle unnoticed. It was not to be, however, for about 2.00 P.M. the smoke and gunfire grew spotty and we could see and be seen more clear, and I thought, I have surely brought my pigs to a pretty market if I get among those ships after they cease fighting. And then came a puff of stronger wind more from the west and we were suddenly in the midst and a part of sights and sounds and happenings beyond belief. The sea about us was peppered and pocked with wreckage; every swell as it hove up crested with riven spars, sails, boats, and great ships — some rolling, plunging hulks, some still under command of canvas and rudder, one on fire; and everywhere human bodies — some alive and many, many dreadfully dead.

Here concern for my own neck and the ship and cargo forsook me and I tell thee I was for a time beside myself with anger at man's cruelty and a great pity and desire to help the poor wretches adrift in the terrible disorder. I had our longboat hove out and directed our people who manned her to stand by close aboard us and pick up such as were alive as we might come upon. Also streamed overboard lines, ends of braces, and floats in hopes some might be used by those adrift. By now I had lost count of time and cannot tell thee what we did or how, but sudden out of the confusion our boat was alongside again and we had rigged a gin on larboard main yardarm and were hoisting poor, half-drowned fellows — one a young woman, mother-naked — on deck like jigging mackerel.

In the midst of this a great double-banked barge with a lad in the stern sheets came shooting up on our starboard side and hailed in English, asking to see my manifest. I told him to come aboard and welcome and I would show him, for it was pleasant to hear an English-speaking voice and by his looks he might

42

have been a boy from home. Jumping into our mizzen chains he directed his people to stand by for a hail, and climbing on deck came to attention and asked me if I was the captain of the vessel.

He was desperate quick in his talk and very anxious to know what our lading was. I made out he was a midshipman from H.B.M. Frigate *Euryalus* — Captain Blackwood — and had been dispatched to board us and learn whether we had such cargo as could be useful to the British fleet. I explained, as we were going below, how we were consigned to Leghorn and that I judged I should be held accountable for all goods on board, but he brushed my talk aside and very polite but firm told me to give him my manifest. This done he checked it through, handed it back to me, and hurried on deck again.

Hailing his boat to come alongside he told off ten men and a petty officer to come aboard us — directed me to brace sharp up and, pointing out a great vessel to the north of us that was very much cut up and a wreck so far as spars, ordered me to lay my ship to windward of her and heave to when in that situation, saying his men would assist me to do so with all possible dispatch. Then off he went in his barge to rejoin, as I suppose, the *Euryalus* and report to his captain.

We had no choice that I could see but to obey this youngster's orders, as the hands that had come on board were armed with cutlasses and looked as if they knew how to use them. They were a good crew and gave us a hand to get our longboat on board and fast, coil down our gear towing over side and swing the yards so that we could lay a course for the station indicated. The bo'sun, if that was his title, when I had a chance to talk to him told me that the English under Admiral Lord Nelson's command had well beaten the French and Spanish who had come out of Cadiz the day before and he thought had taken eighteen or twenty prizes and that the ship we were headed for was the *Royal Sovereign* with Admiral Collingwood, second in command, on board her.

It was getting toward late afternoon when we reached our station and I had a spell when I could look about. While everywhere seemed destruction and confusion at first, I assure thee I could see that the English were making well-ordered progress toward securing the prizes they had taken and saving all lives they could, now that their enemies had ceased to resist. Boats were passing in all directions and all English vessels were swarming with hands repairing damage — and all this work going forward in spite of the ever growing swell, the forerunner of a gale of wind.

The sun as he sank lower broke through the clouds for a time and lit up everything with a red glare. A ship well to leeward and some north of us blew up in a tower of flame and a noise like the trump of doom. I confess to thee I felt homesick then and prayed that I might come safe out of this clinch I'd fallen into, but before I could pity myself too much a half dozen boats came alongside and two officers boarded us and made themselves known. They first thanked me for saving such people as I had and transferred them to their flotilla. They then told me it was reported Lord Nelson had died of wounds received early in the engagement, and handed me a document ordering me — but very polite — to deliver all my deals, staves, parcels of oak timber, apples, tobacco, and certain of the flour lading, "to H.B.M.'s fleet, Admiral Collingwood in command, off Cape Trafalgar, Spain, this twenty-first day October, A.D. 1805."

I asked them how I was to get my pay for all this and was told I should retire to the cabin with one of them and arrive at a fair bargain while the other would supervise the discharge of the articles listed. There was no doubt they meant business and were in a hurry, and being powerless to resist I gave orders to our crew to open the hatches and to tally with the English as cargo was discharged into the boats. I found my man fair and reasonable, and when we had struck a price on the items he explained that we should go on board the Admiral where the paymaster of the fleet would settle with me. I would tell thee these gentlemen's names, but I was so bustled and disturbed in all these transactions that I have forgot them if, as I suspect, they told me.

When our business was over we went on deck to find the discharging of our holds proceeding like clockwork, and not long after that I found myself in the stern sheets of one of the British boats racing down alongside the great three-decker [*Royal Sovereign*] that lay plunging and wallowing in the swell. She was painted yellow in broad bands with black ports which gave her a checkered appearance, all smoked and scorched like a lamp chimney with untrimmed wick, and everywhere gouged and splintered and stove in. As she rolled away from us her new coppered bottom would heave out and I could see where she'd received shots below the water line and must be leaking very considerable. We had to jump for it to get onto her Jacob's ladder as both the boat and she lay so uneasy. We boarded her through a port on the deck above the orlop. Here indeed were the infernal regions. Gear of all sorts smashed and splintered, spills of blood underfoot, sour-smelling powder smoke drifting in layers, but mercifully for me all was dim and the crew in squads driving on their various work in a wonderfully ordered fashion. Every plank and timber in the ship was squawking and groaning, and overall I could hear pumps working full bore.

No time for looking about was given me as I was bustled through, over and around to a berth lit by candles in the stern where an officer and a crew of clerks were very busy with books and papers. Here after considerable formalities between my two officers and the paymaster I was identified and tallies presented with prices against the items. A clerk made up the total, which was submitted to me and if correct asked to receipt.

This done, another clerk counted out six canvas bags which I was told contained £500 each and I was handed still another bag with the odd amount counted into it in gold and silver to bring up the sum required. My conductors told off the squad of men they'd brought with them; my money bags were picked up, the paymaster shook my hand, and off we marched to board the boat again. As I went down the side I wondered how in all this confusion my pay would fare and I was not easy in my mind about it until I was back again on the deck of my own ship with all seven of the bags beside me.

One of my good friends (for by now I felt the two officers were friends) had not left the flagship with us, but the other was still along and came on board the *Ann* in order that he might get my receipt for the safe delivery of the specie, all very regular and well-ordered and showed what wonderful discipline and good feeling existed throughout this British fleet, and when I expressed my astonishment was told that there was not a man high or low in the thousands in the British navy but would cheerfully lay down his life to please and oblige Lord Nelson, who had just given his life to save them all from the clutches of "Boney."

With his receipt buttoned into the pocket of his tight uniform coat my friend thanked me in the name of the Admiral for my compliance with their requests, told me in his opinion a SW gale was brewing up, that our position was six leagues W by N of Cape Trafalgar, and shaking my hand and advising me to get offshore on the larboard tack jumped into his boat and was gone in the darkness which had now fallen.

I can tell thee I took that advice to get offshore as there was every sign of bad weather nearby. There was considerable wind from WSW by this time and the great difficulty at first was to keep the ship slowed down in the press of boats and wreckage so as to avoid collisions. By 10.00 P.M. I judged we had made good about five leagues to NW. I owe this to the Almighty who must have had a special eye to our safety. To get out of that battlefield was up helm and down helm, wear and tack in a bad dream of hurry, and growing wind and a heavy sea with lights and boats and hails and gun and rocket signals all around.

We carried lights as ordered by the officers when we left the ship to board the Admiral. This arrangement of lanterns must have been a night signal of the British, for while we were hailed and cursed considerable by boats, we were not ordered to come to and finally worked clear of the whole raffle and could set more sail and begin to get the ship along on desired course. After midnight it blew a gale and from then until eight next morning, we made some progress in a NNW direction under double-reefed topsails and fore-topmast staysail. After this hour it blew so strong we hove her to under close-reefed topsails, main spencer and storm jib.

This gale lasted four days, two of which we spent on larboard tack and two on starboard. The distress this weather must have brought to those battle-torn ships we had so lately seen filled me with a great pity for them and a thankfulness for our comparatively easy situation. Meantime I had opportunity to count my money and found it all in gold coin except for the odd silver to make up my full account. After this, considering the possibility of French privateers boarding us beyond the straits, I hid all ship's treasure in the rudder-trunk by removing and replacing cabin paneling. When this was done I would tell thee of a sudden I felt all abroad my knees went slack and I had a great desire for hot tea, of which I drank many cups, but could not eat until after a long sleep. All hands had the same complaint but on the third day of the gale, with the sharpness of what we'd seen worn off by repose, all our people had recovered to their normal health.

On 10/27 we passed through the Straits with a strong breeze at SW and rain squalls which allowed us to lay our course for this port . . . .

At this point Aunt Lee ceased reading and a healing silence followed. Gradually I became conscious of the gentle hissing of a green log on the fire and the steady ticking of the clock. These sounds seemed to ease the aching tension that had seized me while Captain Snow and the *Ann Alexander* rolled and pitched through the sulphurous hours of that other October afternoon so long ago. But it was not until Aunt Lee had left the room to return presently with the blue jar, and I had a melger slowly dissolving on my tongue, that I came fully awake to the present and the familiar surroundings, while the vividness of suffering bodies "jigged" from great heaving seas faded to less sanguine shades and outline.

Years later — in fact not so long ago — I stood staring up at the stiff effigy of Lord Nelson surveying London from the top of his lofty column — when suddenly, before my astonished eyes, the now almost-forgotten blue jar slowly resolved itself from the soft gray sky until, bulky and clear cut, there it stood aloft, for me the true symbol of Trafalgar.

FOUR

Wind and Wings

I N THE summertime, if the weather was fair, breakfast at
The Cottage was served on the South Terrace. Five strokes
on an old bronze ship's bell (six-thirty, God's time) was the
signal that brought the Skipper and his crew together around
an old pine table.

A wind-twisted buttonwood tree shaded the mossy brick
pavement, while a pergola, over which clambered a wisteria,
still further protected the table against the butter-melting sunshine.

From his seat here the Skipper looked out to the southwest
over Clark's Cove and the Bay beyond and forecast the weather from the sky, wind, and water —and from the evolutions of
the terns and gulls made a shrewd guess as to what schooling
fish, if any, were about. No misinforming daily paper was
required. Sight, sound, and smell supplied all news that was
essential.

One clear, hot morning as we gathered round the table, the
Skipper appeared with a basket of peaches that he had picked

in the walled Peach Alley before the sun could dry the cool night's dew from their soft cheeks, but in whose hearts lay the ardent glow and sweetness of a long procession of sunny days. To peel these thin-skinned beauties we had only to pinch up and break a little fold of the downy envelope, when the whole of it could be stripped off, leaving the pinkish-yellow flesh ready to dissolve, a mouthful of juicy delight, the stone coming away freely without any clinging fibers.

Deborah, nominally the cook but actually the beneficent tyrant of the household, who maintained she could tell from the looks of the sunrise what food would "set tasty" with her "folks," had provided for us that morning a dish of bacon — half fat, half lean, sliced thick (five-eighths of an inch at least), and cooked very slowly in deep bacon fat that had been strained through cheesecloth after trying. The bacon came onto the table enfolded in a napkin, from which it emerged a pale yellow, as free from greasiness and as brittle as a heart of tender young celery — but retaining the full-bodied flavor of Pig.

At sunup that morning in my bedroom, its window overlooking the low kitchen L, I had been awakened by Deborah's voice chanting over and over:

> "Some flour and water and milk of a cow,
> A thousand of licks and a lot of know-how!"

accompanied by the sticky slap, slap, slap of bare palms and the flat side of a butter paddle on a batch of dough. For a full half-hour as I was dressing, "the incomparable Deb" continued these exercises, so I was not in the least surprised or saddened when, flanking the dish of bacon on the tray she set before the Skipper, I saw a Fayal basket heaped with flaky crescents of cinnamon brown, straight from the range oven — favorably known as "Debby's beaten biscuits."

To balance the biscuits was a glass jar of strained lemon-colored honey of last season's "Pepper Bush run." For we "kep" bees at The Cottage, and the Skipper took great pains to cherish a long, thick hedge of clethra at the shaded and damp east bound of one of the meadows. From these graceful spikes of tiny white blooms in August our bees extracted the very essence of all that is most sweet in the New Bedford countryside.

For drink these summer mornings we had tea — Souchong — the color of a lazy, peaty brook, served in small Chinese bowls. As the bowls were filled from a teapot of matching pattern the scalding liquor heated them uncomfortably; so there was a pause that gave time for the thin, smoky steam to whet anticipation to a keen edge and to bring the tea finally to that temperature from which all fiery harshness had disappeared, leaving only, as the first sip met the palate, a flavor of the Far East and an elusive suggestion of Stockholm tar.

In such surroundings, as I spread butter and honey on a succession of beaten biscuits, my mind strayed out and beyond the sparkling ripples on the surface of the distant Bay. Faraway lands had begun to raise their misty mountaintops on my horizons, when the Skipper's excited voice recalled me from my daydreams.

"There they are! They've struck on at last!" And he pointed to the Cove, where a dark shadow was careering over the surface with an armada of terns hovering and diving above it.

The sustained drive and speed of this shadow, the concentration of terns, and the agitated wheeling of a rapidly increasing flock of herring gulls that kept pace with it, all combined to convey a clear message to the Skipper. As he read it, the Bay had been invaded by the ever-hoped-for schools of bluefish, which unpredictably would choose these waters for an attack on the pods of helpless herring fry that always at this season flowed out from certain freshwater streams.

Here was luck for me — something I had waited for all summer. For I had the Skipper's promise that if and when the bluefish struck on, I, as a neophyte, should be inducted into that most exclusive of fraternities, the "Bluefish Trollers" — Dr. Pease (a neighbor on the Point) and the Skipper. Gone were dreams; the glint on the water was not a pathway to future voyaging and adventure, but the arena of the present, where at this very moment was waiting a host of swift and wily adversaries.

Jumping from my chair, I was rushing off to fetch my basket, packed long since with carefully chosen gear, when Eli, Dr. Pease's farm boy, his shirt clinging to his shoulder blades and beads of perspiration glistening on his nose, ran panting onto the terrace to announce:

"Dr. Pease sent me to tell you you'll have to wait for him till he can find out what ails Mis' Bibb — she was took awful bad after breakfast. He give me a dime to tell you you wasn't on no account to go fishin' without him!"

A lurid statement of symptoms followed. Attempted murder by poison was the least I could gather, yet, at the end, the Skipper only sighed, put a coin in the boy's half-extended hand, and said:

"Well! Thank you, Eli, for the message, and here's another dime to run home again and tell the Doctor I'll wait for him — but not one minute past ten — at the boathouse."

Off went Eli and with him my bounding spirits — for, too bad as was the thought that poison had wormed its way into a home on our Point, it was just awful to think that our foray on the bluefish must be postponed for two hours and more. The sun's glory and the splendor of the blue sky seemed dulled, and the hours of daylight stretched ahead drab and dreary as I slumped into my chair again. The thought of the smack boat *Dragon,* all found and ready, waiting interminably at her moorings, almost brought tears to my eyes. Hang it all! Why couldn't Mrs. Bibb choose some other morning to be sick?

"If you'd rather help Deborah make gingerbread than go fishing," said the Skipper suddenly, "get right into the milk room and look hard at a pan of cream — don't waste such a sour face round here! Or — you can look cheerful and help me pick another basket of peaches. They might perk up Mrs. Bibb after the Doctor's doses."

I soon found there was no room in the Peach Alley for such a pest as gloom, and the prospect of being allowed to deliver the basket — an errand of mercy — produced an actual glow of pleasure.

By half-past nine the Skipper and I were at the boathouse with our luncheon in a waterproof bag, the eelskin baits in glass jars of brine, chocked off with hay in a stout splint basket, the hooks and lines looked to, and the water jug rinsed and filled. Again I was beset with impatience and gloom. Suppose the fish took off or Mrs. Bibb died, or a thousand other things went wrong! Even the Skipper's usual calm appeared ruffled by small gusts of temper.

By a quarter to ten the tension was almost unbearable — when suddenly it was released by the sight of an old friend, "Julius Caesar," shuffling through the sandy road toward us, his glossy chestnut hide darkened by sweat, while behind him surged and bobbed a wide-track buggy, its varnished leather hood glistening in the hot sunshine. Abreast of the boathouse the old horse was turned off the road, where he came to a jerky stop in the shade on the north side of the building.

Without a word the Skipper and I laid hold of that rig and had the horse out of the shafts, unharnessed, and the headstall buckled and long hitch rope fast, before Dr. Pease, with empurpled face, could heave his two hundred pounds out of his carriage. Still in silence the three of us, as if our lives depended on it, fell to rubbing down Caesar's coat with wisps of hay from a burlap sack that was lashed to the rear "ex," and it was not until Caesar had given himself a shivering shake of contentment and a feed of hay had been spread at his forefeet, that the Doctor, mopping his own face and heavy black side whiskers with his bandanna, broke into speech. "Jehosophat!" said he. "That was a close shave!"

This remark, although I wondered whether it referred to Mrs. Bibb, or the time, or to some event on the road, was entirely disregarded by the Skipper, as with irritable energy he hustled us aboard the *Dragon,* to have her presently under sail, heading for the open water of the Bay. Out there the fresh southwest wind, which had overcome the land breeze of early morning, gave the *Dragon* her top range of mobility, while the clear atmosphere allowed the Skipper to keep in constant sight of his scouts, the squadrons of terns, on whose evolutions he so largely based his maneuvers in his battles with the fish. Besides the terns there were flocks of gulls to be watched and also a fleet of twenty or more boats to be kept so far as possible at a distance.

"No living creature — not even a fish — likes to be disturbed at mealtimes," was a saying the Skipper kept in mind when he designed his fishing boat, the *Dragon.* She was eighteen feet overall with a beam of six and a half feet, had a low freeboard, and was undecked except for narrow waterways and washboards. A crew of three was her limit without overcrowding. If properly sailed she made little disturbance forward or aft, and her low sides made for ease in getting fish inboard quickly and quietly.

The fishlines, or drails, as we called them, were cotton, three-strand, nine-thread, with a hard twist, and about the size of a cod line. A single steel hook scraped bright, the point and barb filed sharp to cope with the well-armed and armored mouth of the bluefish, was attached to the drail with a three-ply twisted copper wire leader, on which was threaded a long bead of lead, also scraped bright. An eelskin inside out was stretched over this combination and so lashed that the bright hook, as it was towed, could wiggle freely, somewhat after the manner of a sand eel's tail, while the shining bead suggested his head.

Our stations and duties aboard the boat that day were: Dr. Pease as ballast in the waist, to windward, tending a two-hundred-foot drail; I on the lee side in charge of a longer line;

the Skipper aft with no line, but both hands busy with the tiller and sheet of the loose-footed, untanned spritsail — his faculties on the stretch to put the Doctor and me over the belated stragglers of the driving schools, which take a bait more eagerly than the leaders of the van.

To head off a school of bluefish was unprofessional. To be caught in a jam of boats was to be branded a "bungler"; but to outguess competitors by observation of the terns' actions was to the Skipper an art that seemed to give him more than half his pleasure in this sort of fishing. Nevertheless it was serious business, and the *Dragon* was a silent ship, except for the Skipper's frequent warnings of "Hard-a-lee!" or "Jibe-oh!" — and the flip and flatter of a landed fish and the splashing as it was tossed into the fish-well abaft the centerboard trunk.

So occupied, time slipped quickly by, until suddenly the day seemed to pause — the blue of the sky to windward paled to gray, the fish took off, and the wind lost some of its vigor.

"Time to reel up!" said the Skipper as he noted this lull and realized that the fish-well was nearly full, while his own "innards" felt empty.

As the lines came inboard to be faked neatly on their square hardwood reels, the *Dragon* was put sharp on the wind, and presently came to anchor in the lee of White Rock, with the sail frapped round the mast and stopped with several turns of the sheet.

While the grub and the wadded basket with its pot of hot tea were being dug out of the stern locker, the eelskins were peeled off the hooks and sealed in the jars of brine, and the hooks given a wipe with a tallowed rag.

Lying there in the cool shadow of the big pink granite rock, the *Dragon* was rolled gently by the little swell that swashed against the rock's sheer base, while her crew relished their sandwiches of toasted rye bread, cold roast beef, and raw tomatoes.

Sleep undoubtedly would have followed, had not a pod of herring fry, looking more like a chunk of pressed Smyrna dates than a school of fish, floated slowly upward alongside.

Instantly the *Dragon* became a ringside seat at an exhibition that far outdid any man-made spectacle. For suddenly from the depths shot scores of bluefish — a steel-blue flotilla of nature's submarines, murderous action personified — that tore into that huddle of innocence, ripping and slashing as it passed and leaving a wake of wreckage behind, while, timed to a split second, the air above was alive with heavy-winged herring gulls that swooped down to come to rest on the water, head to wind, and fall to work gobbling up the maimed survivors of the attack, now drifting helplessly on the surface.

Above the gulls was a ceiling of terns, more numerous and incredibly swift, attacking the pod that still floated aimlessly a few inches underwater. Shimmering like glazed porcelain when touched by the sunbeams and filling the air with their creaking cries, the terns wheeled, hovered, dipped, and rose till, their objective marked, they dove like bullets, to disappear below the surface and reappear as quickly, each with a fishlet in its orange-red, black-tipped beak.

The concentration of such number of these aerial acrobats gave the feeling of being in the midst of a furiously agitated storm cloud that was tossed about in uttermost confusion and from which fell a silvery rain that purfled the sea with countless dimples, but of which not one drop landed on the *Dragon* or collided one with another. Of all his acts, the most skillful is that by which the tern, emerging from his dive, withdraws himself from the rain of his fellows. Mathematically, it would seem impossible for a body of his size and shape to come to the surface, spread his wings, project himself into the air with head to wind, and instantly select a course clear of his companions, who are showering down seemingly into the same spot he but that instant has quitted.

Then, as mysteriously as it had appeared, the pod of fry sank, the air above the *Dragon* was wiped clear of terns, and the only evidence of such murderous combat was a gull or two, lifting and falling on the gentle swell, mopping up what was left of the carnage.

But if, as the Skipper pointed out, the sky was searched, a steady drift of terns could be seen on a northeasterly course at a height of perhaps forty to sixty feet, while another ragged procession was flying out to windward — or southwest — so close to water level as to appear at times to pass through rather than over a wave. Those aloft were flying light; those below were carrying every one a silvery fry.

After watching these hard-working birds for a while, the Doctor said: "If it's agreeable to you, Skipper, I'd jest as soon cruise about for a spell watchin' the birds and tryin' to drive some sense into this blame' boy's head."

The "blame' " boy showed that *he* was agreeable to the Doctor's proposal by twitching the grapnel off the bottom smartly, while the Skipper unfurled the sail, shoved the sprit into its becket on the mast, and began to jog the *Dragon* slowly to windward.

From the spate of information that now poured forth, I gathered that the birds on the southwest course were grownups who'd been to market and were hurrying home with their supplies to feed their ever-hungry fledglings, which nestled on a barren islet six miles to windward, known as "Gull Island" — the then, and present, summer resort of tern society; further, that they were flying as close to the surface as they could to take advantage of the "drag" the water creates on the lower hem of the wind that passes over it. Obvious too, was the fact that this drag which brakes the wind extends upwards only a few inches on a windy day, while on a calm one, particularly when a strong tidal current is running counter to the direction of the wind, this influence stretches many feet aloft and is often powerful enough to appear to kill what little breeze is astir.

And now, as sometimes happens of a summer afternoon on Buzzards Bay, the southwest wind faltered and gradually dropped to a calm. Within a half hour the warmth died out of the air, followed by a cool breath from the east, tainted with a hint of clammy mudflats. Close on the heels of this herald came a light northeast breeze, bringing with it a rose-pearl fog that slowly enveloped the *Dragon,* until she was sailing alone and silent inside a contracted sphere of mist and gray-green water.

During this shift of weather I had not been allowed to sit idle with heedless eyes; for again the Doctor gave all his attention to "driving sense in," and before the fog shut down too thickly I had seen the procession of birds, beating their way close along the wavetops to the island, suddenly rise to take the upper track, while those coming to market dropped to the lower one — a complete reversal of conditions earlier in the day. Watching the homegoers sailing high with hardly moving pinions, it was beyond doubt that they had found the exact height at which the new, favorable wind gave them the maximum of speed with the least effort, and that the travelers below had gauged to an inch the level where the drag cut to its limit the countercurrent of air.

With visibility contracted to a few yards by the fog, I became fearful that my interesting friends, the terns, would lose their way, leaving the "chickens" on the island to starve. In a whisper I confided this fear to the Doctor — but he only shook his head and pointed astern, where, looking like gray ghosts with black caps, tern after tern shot out of the smoking wall to leeward and disappeared to windward in the blink of an eye. Every tern so seen, ahead or astern, cut the boat's course at the same angle. There was no sign of confusion in his flight; every move was purposeful. He was confidently on his desired course.

By early evening the Skipper had piloted the *Dragon* safely through the fog to her moorings and landed his crew in the boathouse.

Here he and the Doctor, after rolling up their shirt sleeves and tying on their oilskin aprons, were about to operate on the row of ten plump bluefish, the pick of the *Dragon*'s well, that lay before them on the skinning bench, and the Doctor had actually made his first incision when the Skipper, suddenly paling at the tearing sound of the stroke, dropped his knife and cried:

"Good Lord, Lem! — What about Mrs. Bibb? I never thought about the poor woman all day. What ailed her, and did she die?"

"Poison — not dead," replied the Doctor.

A long pause followed while the Skipper's curiosity built itself up until he exploded with:

"Oh, come on, now! Tell us what you did for her."

"Nothin' very much," said the Doctor mildly. "Jest watched her for a while, and when I seen she was a-sinkin' and a-sinkin', says I to myself, 'That woman's got sunthin' inside her what had oughter come out' — so I pumped her out."

The Doctor's subdued tone, and the astoundingly graphic picture he drew, so stimulated my imagination that I stood staring at him, pale and shivering. Divining my distress and need of more enlightenment, he continued: " 'Twa'n't nothin' but white powder — arsenic, I suspicion. Arsenic's kinder easy to get mixed into the sugar bowl 'most anywheres. Don't need to worry none about it — bound to happen in the best of families oncet in a while."

And with that he turned to the work in hand, leaving me then and forever after somewhat suspicious of sugar bowls in general, but positively distrustful of those in the "best families."

FIVE

Islands

ABUILDING with the figures "1801" cut into a jamb of a doorframe still stands at the head of one of the wharves in New Bedford. Its walls of rough-cut, pinkish granite are thirty inches thick, so well and carefully laid up in tempered lime-and-sand mortar that so far they have defied the building wrecker. The "Candle Works" is too solidly put together to pay the cost of demolition.

The site on which this veteran rests was scooped out of a hillside, with the result that the north and east walls rise a clear three stories above the wharf level, while the west wall tops the land by only one story and the pitch of the roof. The south wall is compensated to the natural, untouched slope of the hill, and the three entrance doors on its face are approached by steps of roughly dressed stone that vary in number from two at the west to a long flight at the shoreward end.

It is evident that this stubborn old pile was so constructed to ease the labor of rolling casks and barrels into it from the wharf, and by its partially underground character to hold the sperm oil in these containers at an even temperature in all seasons.

Here in the dim-lit, cavernous workrooms spermaceti candles were made, of a quality so superior they had gradually come to command a world-wide market. Packed in stout wooden boxes lined with blue paper they had the appearance of cores cut from blocks of pure Carrara marble. After long voyaging great numbers of them came to stand — slim guardians in snowy white — shedding their soft mellow radiance over Christian altars both stately and humble in lands far distant from their birthplace.

Years ago I came to know the Candle Works intimately; for it was in the west end of it the Skipper maintained his counting room, or office, in chambers partitioned off from the workrooms by white pine paneling that time had tinged to old ivory. A handsome cast-iron stove with a firebox of sufficient size to digest full-length cordwood logs so stood that, with the help of a long brass smoke pipe, the rooms were pleasantly warmed on the coldest days of winter.

At a tall, highly polished mahogany desk stood Chris Harrington, the thin, gray-bearded clerk, ever busy making entries in calf-bound ledgers or journals. To protect him from the rub of the desk-edge he wore around his middle a short apron of tough green baize, while long arm guards of plaited straw protected his shirt sleeves from soil and wear. Like the stove, the stout wooden-seated chairs, the Skipper's knee-hole bureau, the heavy round table of black walnut, the two half models of the ships *George and Susan* and *George Howland* clamped on the chimney breast, Chris, standing there at his desk, was an integral part of the counting room.

There was one other piece of animate furniture on these premises — Cotton Bole, a bent and wizened Barbadian Black, whose bald crown was framed by a fringe of white wool. With a duster of turkey feathers in one hand and dustpan and brush in the other, he was constantly on the move about the rooms, beating off the attacks of dirt and dust and rubbing off the corruption of rust and tarnish. Tucked under the leather belt around his waist were cloths for polishing and scrubbing, so that no surface that would take a shine failed to receive attention as he passed. The brass balls capping the four corners of the stove shone so brilliantly they dazzled the dullest eye. But like all perfectionists Cotton Bole had to face the unattainable in one detail — for, do what he might, he could never rid the counting room of a slight but not altogether unpleasant odor of sperm oil seeping through the partitions from the other parts of the old building.

There came a time when on winter afternoons of thaw or rain, with no skating or coasting available, I would hurry to the Candle Works as soon as lunch at home was over; for there, hanging on the walls of the counting room, were many prints and paintings by "Uncle Ben" Russell and other marine artists, which by their prodigious and accurate detail defied all efforts to exhaust their interest. "The Ship *Corinthian* in tow of the Ship *George Howland* in the Arctic" — a Russell, and so far as I have been able to discover the only imprint made of this particular lithograph — was the gem of the collection. The transparent greens of the ice, the frosty sparkle of the snow, the olive tint in the water, the sharpness of every line and curve gave to this portrait of the ships and their situation and surroundings a reality and vividness beyond compare. It was as if I had witnessed this very scene — when, presto! The frost had preserved and locked it complete and forever in my memory. It was from hours of study of these pictures and Cotton Bole's professional knowledge of nautical detail that I came to read *Two Years Before the Mast* and other sound accounts of sea life with understanding and delight.

One rainy afternoon in February, at the Skipper's suggestion, Cotton Bole, armed with a bunch of big brass keys and a whale-oil bull's-eye lantern, piloted me through the door leading from the counting room to the other parts of the Candle

Works, which up to this time I had never visited. As we groped our way through cool, dark spaces the blob of our light began to reveal treasures that to my eyes dwarfed those of the mines of Golconda, about which I had heard so much from Cousin Neal, a Calcutta merchant. There were few traces of candle-making now, for that business had faded away years before I came on the scene. Instead, the place was packed with ships' gear and curios gathered from all the Seven Seas. On the ground-level floor we found an Eskimo kayak, west coast of Greenland model — sealskin stretched over bone and drift-wood frame — hanging from the oil-soaked timbers of the floor above. She was complete, with double paddle, boot, har-poon, bladder, and lines — a masterpiece of her kind, which I instantly coveted. Nearby, hanging like great bats, were suits of Arctic waterproof — jumpers and pantaloons — made of the intestines of whales and, though now dried out and brittle, still smelling to heaven. At the head of one of the ladder-like stair-ways I was startled by coming face to face with an upreared polar bear, whose long white teeth and glassy eyes gleamed lifelike in the lantern light, though when I came to run my hand down his shaggy sides he turned out to be dreadfully moth-eaten and dusty. To find him so harmless and neglected was anticlimax. But after we'd climbed to the attic, and Cotton Bole had sprayed his light over the walls and floor to expose a brass-bound mahogany sea chest and several tiers of smaller pine boxes painted green with white lettering on them, I felt the rapture of the lone prospector who discovers new country or precious ore; for on lifting the lid of the chest, I saw lying there a great collection of whale ivory scrimshaw work. Here were miniature tackle blocks, single, double, and even treble, sheaves, pins, strops, and all; fids of all sizes; serving mallets; jagging wheels for crimping the edges of piecrusts; spoons, forks, sailmakers' hearts, thimbles, and rings; toys and puzzles; yarn reels, line reels, net-makers' shuttles — enough to keep me busy for days examining and appraising — and all with

63

that patina which gives to hand-carved bone a quality delighting the fingertips. And when I came to look into a few of the smaller green boxes to find them stuffed with old documents and letters, on many of which were postage stamps and franks from ports in China, Japan, Mauritius, St. Helena, Cape Colony, Archangel, and islands and countries of which I had never heard, I, as a budding philatelist, was stricken dumb by the thought of the riches stowed away here in this old attic.

The upshot of this first exploration was that the Skipper gave me the run of the Candle Works, "with this understanding — that no single thing is to find its way into your pockets or be shifted from its place." And so for a while I spent every spare hour I could — mostly in the attic — with the lantern and an old blue-backed chart of the Pacific, until I had a fair working acquaintance with the names of the innumerable islands and their groupings in that vast ocean. Cape Horn in spite of its stormy reputation came to beckon with all the allure of a siren who could lead me to the palmy gardens of the Hesperides. And when in a box marked "United States Guano Co." I found a long account of a tiny dot on the chart designated as "Howland Island," I rushed down to the counting room to interrupt the Skipper with a flood of questions about this, as I assumed, family possession. To have an interest, even if it turned out to be a small one, in a tropic island deep in the Pacific (49'N., 176°-43'-23"W.) would be fortune beyond all imagining. I fairly fizzed with excitement.

After patiently hearing me out, the Skipper, instead of answering my questions, said:

"Now, old man, I'll tell you what you do: Be here at twelve-thirty sharp next Saturday noontime to have lunch with me and some old friends of the 'Codfish Club' — and try to have clean hands and nails and your hair and clothes all shipshape — and I think perhaps you'll get some of the information you're after."

When Saturday came round at last, big wet flakes of falling snow were plastering the weather sides of buildings and trees and turning to slush as they came to ground. As I sloshed along over the slippery pavements on my way to the Candle Works, the northeast wind cut through my waterproofs to chill me to the marrow. The allure of tropic isles weakened, while the pull of that great stove in the counting room grew; so that when I arrived at the glossy black door with its brass knob, I was ahead of time. Opening the door, I ran into Cotton Bole waiting in the entry to brush me down and take charge of my galoshes, "so's you won't traipse no street litter onto my clean floors"; after which attentions I was allowed to pass into the warmth and order beyond.

I found the Skipper alone in his room unpacking a hamper he had brought from The Cottage that morning when he had driven up to town. He was too busy arranging the contents on his big round table to do more than nod to me at first; but presently handing me a stack of plates he said: "Bear a hand with these and put 'em in the rack on the stove where they can get a-warming."

Coming back from this errand in the outer office, I was told to set the silver and glasses for five places while the Skipper lighted the four burners of a spirit lamp under a tin-lined copper chafing dish. As soon as steam began to puff out from the water bath he picked up an olivewood salad spoon and began to charge the dish with a couple of pounds, perhaps, of boned and flaked salt codfish, which, soaked in fresh water overnight, had been brought to a boil before leaving The Cottage. Into the pan with the fish went six boiled potatoes — fluffy and white as applewood ash — an equal number of boiled globe onions, and a small bowlful of finely diced and boiled crimson beets. Kneading and mixing this combination with his spoon, the Skipper presently began to temper it generously with medium white sauce — smooth and lumpless as mayonnaise — and dabs of mustard worked into a dun-colored paste with tarragon vinegar and ground turmeric. When the batter began to steam two hard-boiled eggs were added, and finally, after twenty minutes, one raw egg to smooth it out went in to be absorbed into the pink-tinged creamy mash. The odor which now pervaded the room vanquished the outer dreariness of the snow-drenched day; spring seemed close by.

As the minute hand of the banjo clock between the two ship models came to the half-hour mark, Cotton Bole threw open the door to the outer office to announce with a welcoming flourish of his arm: "Cap'ns Pope, Reynard, and Wasque come aboard, Sah!" — and presently I was being introduced as "Matthew Howland's grandson."

To meet and be about to sit at the table with three such seasoned and successful deep-sea captains was an experience to quite bowl me over, and I felt so small and insignificant that, when Captain Pope held my hand in his great sun-glazed paw and said: "We ought to be friends, my boy — for I've made four voyages for your grandfather, three in the old *Russo (Rousseau)* and one in *Desdemona*," I felt I was being greeted by the "Old Man of the Mountain," as I looked up into a face so obviously sculptured from a block of New Hampshire granite — scored deep by icy gales. And throughout the time I was in their company that day this mood of awed fascination held me speechless and spellbound.

At this moment Cotton Bole came in again from the outer room with the hot plates and a half-dozen of White Label Bass Ale, cool from the cellar; and we sat down to table, the Skipper with the chafing dish before him. One after another he heaped the plates with smoking batter, capping each with a spoonful of crisp salt-pork "scraps" fresh from Deborah's try-kettle that very morning. Until this first helping had disappeared and a glass of ale with it, there was little or no conversation. But with a second help all round, the Skipper, looking at Captain Reynard, said:

66

"This boy here's been pestering me with questions about Cape Horn, and you know I've only passed by there once on my way home from the East — and we weren't lingering any. How about telling him of those days down there sealing in the schooner *Willie* of Noank, when you were a youngster?"

And so it came about that, while I, too keen to eat, watched the others "lick the platter clean," Captain Reynard — as his named implied, agile, neat, and sagacious as a New England dog fox — steered us through the labyrinth of waterways lying between Magellan Straits and Diego Ramirez Rocks — the most southerly outposts of the Americas. We lay with him aboard the *Willie* all snug in landlocked harbors while summer gales screamed overhead among the jagged teeth of the sheer rock mountains of Magallanes. We followed him sure-footedly, shod with rope-soled canvas boots, over boulders and ledges slippery with thin summer moss and mildew. We shot strange game; we took a few seals, skinned 'em, and cured the pelts. And on our way to the Falkland Islands we rode great seas — "Cape Horn Graybeards" — as buoyant and dry in the little schooner as the albatross which kept us company on his ten-foot spread of wings. In Port Stanley we came to know that king of the South Atlantic, Captain Smiley, a native of Providence, Rhode Island — and his lovely little yacht-like brig. And at last, after a voyage of some eight hundred miles "to the east and a bit south," with the fogs and cold rains of the Falklands behind us, we raised the ten-thousand-foot peaks of South Georgia.

"You can cut out all the other islands in the world," said the Captain as he came to this point in his narration. "None of 'em can hold a candle to South Georgia for takin' the breath out of you with the sheer savage thrust of those tawny, snow-patched mountains towerin' up 'most to the zenith and every fang of 'em traced clear against the blue of a summer sky."

It took us the best part of a day with a good breeze astern before we came abreast of the roots of those immense heights, and the clear ink-blue of the offshore water shifted to Chinese green, with a curdle of white where it churned against the rocky walls. Great patches of snow lying in the hollows aloft were "packin' and workin' " — turning into rivers of ice "weavin' and pitchin' " down tremendous drops to end in cliffs of light blue overhangin' the sea." These falls of ice were so high we lay on our backs on deck "to ease the cramp in our necks" as we stared up to the tops of them, while great chunks "the size of the Spring Street Meetin' House" dropped off into deep water with a "whop like a tremendous school o' right whales lashin' out with their flukes." When we came to "a narrow break in the face of the rock and no bottom with the lead, and the wind cut off so 'twas glassy calm ahead," we "out with the sweeps" and rowed the *Willie* into a deep bight — right up to the head of it — where again we got no bottom and had to moor her fore and aft with lines and anchors ashore jammed among boulders and shingle. "It was almighty still in there except for an occasional grumble from shiftin' ice 'way aloft and the distant sneezin' and roarin' of herds of sea elephants that had hauled ashore for family purposes in among the thin grass and moss that made a green streak in places between the beach and the foundation of the mountain." And when the short Antarctic night settled down we felt small — "small as red ants crawlin' round on the stone doorstep at home in Westport."

"And talk about climate and spicy, sweet-smellin' breezes," concluded Captain Reynard, "there's none I ever sampled or snuffed so upliftin', so clean and fresh as a summer westerly spell brings to that country down there — if you're nineteen with a stream of good red blood racin' round inside you."

At this I felt, rather than heard, a little regretful sigh escape from the four men while the impression of those remote, windswept wildernesses soaked in. And then the Skipper said:

"Well, when you're nineteen there are mighty few places in this world you can find much fault with — if they're new to you. But I remember three months on Oahu that I wouldn't swap for Heaven, when I lived at the Cartwrights' plantation

house up in the hills and rode down to Honolulu in the mornings and back again in the evenings. There was a little swift
stream of clear water ran right through that part of the house I
was quartered in, with a huge Chinese bowl — six by three, by
two-and-a-half-foot deep — all glazed with pinks and greens
and sunk into the bed of the brook. Whenever I'm hot and
sweaty now I pine for that bowl with the cool water running
through it in little silvery whirlpools and threads of current. A
bath there before meals came to mean as much and more than
the cool ripe melons and the curried chicken and rice and so
many other tropical delicacies Mrs. Cartwright tempted us
with as we sat at dinner on the lanai, where we could look out
over miles of mountain country and sea.

"The air up there had the quality of rubbing all the rough
spots out of you so that, no matter how troublesome the business of the day down below had been, you'd soon be content
and happy to watch the sunset, with the valleys turning misty
purple and the mountain peaks to gold. And on a night of full
moon with the sea spread out below us, alive and dancing in
silver and black, it seemed we heard the steady rhythm of the
universe with the wind, surf, leaves, grass, and even the stars,
each and all playing their part in concert with the others — and
that," said he to me, "is the best I can do for you, old man —
with the one and only Pacific island I've lived on."

"God a'mighty, Skipper!" piped up little Captain Wasque.
"Do you want to get rid o' this boy of yours, enticin' him with
yarns such as yourn and Cap'n Reynard's? Now look here, Bub,
you listen to me some — an' I'll learn you to think settin' right
here in the Candle Works ain't such a bad way to go cruisin'.
There's islands in the Pacific would make Hell look like the
Garden of Eden 'fore Adam fell, an' one of 'em I got too well
acquainted with is in the Galapagos. When I begun my sea-
farin' it warn't unusual to put into that archipelago o' cinders to
lay in a store o' them big turtles that'll stay alive in prime
condition six months without food or water. They was cheap

69

vittles and drink — the sweet water in the big bags inside 'em bein' tastier than stale water from casks.

"I was cook aboard the *St. George* the night we lay there anchored, all snug, in four fathoms, with Albemarle Island on one hand an' Narborough on t'other. We was all below asleep, for there warn't a breath stirrin' an' no company. Sudden, without no warnin', there come an explosion that blew us out o' our berths an' bounced us on deck with our hearin' gone for the time bein' — an' there on our starboard hand was Albemarle Island vomitin' its red-hot innards into high heaven, with great slabs o' the mountainside meltin' an' fallin' down into the sea. There was another explosion that knocked us all flat, an' when we was on our feet again there was a roarin' river o' lava pourin' into the bay up to north'ard of us — the water fizzin' an' crackin' like salvos o' naval cannon. We was so took up watchin' this fireworks we made no special account o' our own situation 'til it begun to grow intoler'ble hot, an' the pitch meltin' in the deck seams warned us the ship was feelin' it too.

"Cap'n Barker, sensin' we was in a tight box, an' hopin' a breeze would make up to move us, had us heave short on the anchor an' set all workin' sail. But, no wind comin', there we lay 'till noon next day, by which time the tar'd all melted out o' the standin' riggin', the paint all blistered an' peelin', an' we so wilted we hadn't the strength to lower a boat an' try to tow her off. An' all that time that mountain, fifteen mile or more to the north'ard, kep' spewin' red-hot rivers into the bay, with the temperature of the water climbin' 'til it was considerable over 100°. 'Twas almost as black as night overhead, with the most tremendous tempest o' thunder an' lightnin' I ever see. Just when most o' the crew thought we was cooked gooses, there come a puff o' wind from the east'ard — then another an' another, 'til there was a good light breeze. We could jest muster enough beef to back the headsails an' get way on her so's to trip the anchor an' make off from that Hell's chimbley. 'Twas most an hour 'fore we had spunk enough to heave in that chain an' cat the anchor. When we got a good offin' some forty miles to the sou'west we hove her to — an' even at that distance we could see them flames an' hear the boomin'.

"*No, sir!* there's only two kinds of islands in the Pacific an' both of 'em good for nothin' — them as has mountains waitin' to bust out an' burn ye alive an' them as has coral reefs an' red-hot beaches where there's nothin' to do an' where you'll drown to death if a hurricane comes along — which it most gen'ally does when you're there. If you want islands, give me them right here to home — Naushon an' Hadley Harbor for choice — on a clear October evenin' where you can turn in without no volcanoes an' coral strands layin' uneasy on your mind."

While the other three had been opening up new horizons for me, Captain Pope had sat immovable and silent as the rock he so resembled. But now, with the conclusion of Captain Wasque's florid testimony, he rolled his cigar with his lips from one corner of his mouth to the other and, pinning my attention with a glance from his compelling gray eye, he rumbled into speech:

"Islands — and I've seen a good few in my thirty years at sea — home ones and distant ones, are all alike in one particular; there's water all 'round 'em. Other than this no two are just the same and most all I've set foot on were interesting, one way or another, and worth the trouble of getting to 'em. But there is one I came to know well — and it's tropic all right, and a long way from home, too — that took a lot of time and trouble to find; and any way you look at it, it's *no account.* It's called 'Howland Island,' and lays right on the Line, and almost to the 180th meridian in the Pacific."

Here I felt the Skipper eyeing me, while my ears began to burn at the thought of the family name attaching to property of such shameful character. It was a painful awakening after a delightful dream. I sat rigid, staring at Captain Pope as he continued:

" 'Twas October, '53, I was instructed right here in the Candle Works to sign on an old Quaker gentleman named Cobleigh for a voyage in the *Russo,* and to put him ashore on Howland

Island when convenient so that he could investigate and make a report on what he found there.

"Within a week of our sailing in October I found he was real good company, and before he'd left the ship in Honolulu, in July, '54, I'd come to think the world of him. He was plumb full of information about plants and trees and birds and that sort of thing — and patient, too — never pestered me to push along for the Island when we were spending three months off the coast of Peru taking some eighteen hundred barrels of sperm oil between 10° and 20° South and 100° and 120°, so that it was somewhere about the thirtieth of May, '54, when we finally found that little spit of coral sand with a thick crust of bird droppings on top, baked hard by the sun.

"Two hours ashore there with Friend Cobleigh was enough for me, and it was a week before I could relish my vittles after the smell of that hen-run. But Cobleigh, though I could see he was almighty disappointed — the island was barren and only a mile and a quarter long by about a half mile across — went ashore there every day for ten days and I guess there wasn't a foot of it he didn't go over with a fine-tooth comb.

"I came to hate that dump of sand, it seemed so lonely and forlorn, but wicked too; for it was all ringed 'round by coral reefs with only one break on the westerly side that a shallow draft boat could wriggle through, and sixty fathom and more of water right off the edges of the reefs, making it too deep to lay to an anchor, so we had to jog-jog day after day watching the weather, ready to clear out in a hurry if it came on to blow.

"Being not more than twenty foot above sea level at any point, that island's a perfect trap to catch a vessel off her course some dark rainy night, and that must have happened long before Captain Netcher first reported it in '41; for, besides the thousands of birds making it their headquarters, there were armies of rats — almost more of 'em than birds. Friend Cobleigh figured they were Scandinavian ship rats, and that they'd been there long enough to have lost any fear of folks; for when I was ashore with him we scuffed through bands of 'em like dead leaves in autumn at home. How they made out to live there was a mystery to Cobleigh; for there was nothing for 'em to eat except eggs and fledglings, for which he figured they had to fight the old birds. And when it came to fresh water, all he could discover was what an occasional shower might drop on that sizzling crust. Hard pickings, we thought; and yet there they were — myriads of 'em — and they gave the old gentleman and Cotton Bole here a couple of bad nights, when they were ashore one noontime and it came up to blow sudden and hard, so that I had to make an offing and leave 'em there. We'd drifted seventy-five miles or more to the southeast before that blow quit, and it took us forty-eight hours in the doldrums that followed to work up to the Island again.

"By the time we'd fetched those two aboard ship they were all through with Howland Island, for good and *all* — and I don't blame 'em; for it seems that very first night the rats must have smelled some scraps and crumbs of the cold vittles they had with 'em, and swarmed in on where they lay sheltering from the wind. At last they got gallied, the vermin were so thick, and they began to fight 'em. The minute they'd clubbed a few, more rats than ever began to move in to eat their dead relations, and Mr. Cobleigh and Cotton Bole took to their heels and had to keep on their legs the rest of the night. From then 'til our main royal nicked their horizon, Friend Cobleigh said it was all he could do to fight off the horrors from thinking of those scattered human bones that were discovered on Huafo Island, which was infested with rats same as Howland. They were as tired a pair as ever I want to see.

"But come to think of it — sitting here all comfortable — Howland Island, with those birds and rats living together on it, was a kind of interesting spot, even if it is no account. And then if we hadn't been fooling 'round there so long we'd never have come across that pair of Kanakas swimming in the middle of nowhere — the man laying on his back with his eyes shut and

73

the woman pushing him along at a good clip on a course for the nearest land, seventy-five miles or more to leeward."

Here, at what seemed to me a most pregnant moment, Captain Pope broke off his tale to select a fresh cigar from the box on the table, clip the end, and light it. The other three, shifting a trifle in their chairs, sat waiting placidly, while I fidgeted impatiently in mine. Then at last, through a cloud of fragrant blue smoke, I heard the deep voice again:

"Finding those two came about this way: Honolulu, where I was to put Friend Cobleigh ashore, lies a scant two thousand miles to the northeast of Howland Island. But to sail there in the *Russo* with the southeast trades to the south'ard of us and the northeast trades to the north'ard, with the doldrums in between, meant we'd got to work considerable of a traverse. So, as soon as Friend Cobleigh was satisfied he had all the information he needed for his report, we started to get the old ship south where we could pick up a westerly and get a push to the east'ard 'til we could fetch to windward of Oahu.

"If you'll believe me, it took the best part of three weeks to work down to where I figured the Tonga Islands bore southeast and the Fijis west and a bit north — with the southeast trades showing signs of quitting.

"Along about nine in the forenoon, while I was working out my time sight for longitude down below, Friend Cobleigh hollered through the skylight there were two seals in sight to windward. Thought I, 'That's impossible in these parts,' but to humor the old man I nipped up on deck to have a look myself, and when I got the glass on 'em I thought for a minute he was right after all. Then those two round, black heads came out sharp on top of a sea and I saw they were two folks swimming, no more than half a mile upwind of us — and the nearest land, one of the Fijis, to the northwest of us. It was something of a startler.

"You can lay we jumped to it to get the main yards aback, way off the ship, and the second mate, Mister Handy's, boat lowered; for I figured those two had been in the water a considerable spell. And I don't think Friend Cobleigh hardly breathed for the twenty minutes until we saw Handy and his crew get those folks safe in board. I know I was pretty impatient myself.

"When the boat was alongside the ship again and before we could give 'em a hand over the rail, those Kanakas — a man and woman, as I've said, and both stark naked — swarmed aboard fresh as spring daisies, all brown and glistening in the sunshine — as fine specimens of humanity as ever I saw, and not a bit put about or flurried, but seeming to take a whole lot of interest in the ship, and all aboard and about her.

"Both of 'em had small leather pouches slung 'round their necks on a bit of string, with a few scraps of breadfruit and dried fish in 'em, which together with their stout hearts and bodies was all the gear they appeared to need for their kind of seafaring.

"After rigging 'em out with some old clothes — and I tell you they strutted — all hands that thought they had any Kanaka talk took a crack at trying to find out how they come to be afloat out there. In the end, Mr. Cobleigh figured the canoe they'd started in from somewhere to windward had fallen apart the day before we come across 'em, so they just naturally kept on with their voyage; which was the right move considering they were about as much at home in the water as on land. The only time they seemed put about was the next day, when we hove to off Tongatabu and invited 'em into the boat to go ashore. There were signs they hankered to stay aboard and continue the voyage with us; but by loading 'em up with odds and ends we finally got rid of 'em all content and happy. Mr. Cobleigh thought it likely they'd start out again soon, and commit barratry in hopes of being picked up. He'd taken a great fancy to 'em and was sorry to see the last of 'em.

"Now of course that isn't much of an adventure to brag about," said the Captain after a short pause, "but whenever I've cruised 'round among those islands in the Pacific I've noticed there'd be some happening out of the ordinary 'most every day; and when Friend Cobleigh read me his report on Howland Island before he left the ship at Honolulu, and among a lot of things I hadn't taken account of he stated there was 125,000 ton of guano lying there for the taking, I came to think perhaps we hadn't wasted time 'round that no-account heap of sand."

Nor did I think I'd wasted my time down there at the Candle Works, as later on that raw evening I ploughed my way home through the slush; for I was dimly aware that within those old stone walls had been born for me a something — call it "that precious seeing of the eye" — which from that day on would endow all islands — for me — far or near, with the charm of magic. And I have proved it so as the years have passed, for, although I have never been so far afloat as my old friends of the Codfish Club, I've seen "a good few of islands — home ones and distant ones," and never without responding to that quality of mystery.

I have even had a feeling in my bones ever since that day that some time Howland Island might emerge from her "no-account" state to stand, proud of her position and name, in the ranks of her sister isles.

And this, too, has come to pass, for, after its many years of lying lonely and neglected, a final disposition has recently been made of that "little spit of coral sand" by the signing of a long-time contract, whereby its value as a steppingstone for trans-Pacific air traffic accrues to and is shared equally by us and the British; stamping it with the distinction of being the first debatable territory on record to be so dealt with — an inspiring augury and precedent in the settlement of international disputes.

SIX

Beetle's

AT THE TIME The Cottage became a second home to me, farming, often including trap-fishing, was the sole industry of Clark's Point — with the exception of the activities at Beetle's Boat Yard.

Here small craft of all kinds were built, among them the "Beetle Whaleboat," so favorably known throughout the sea-going world. As an adjunct to the construction and repair work, a marine railway was in constant operation.

Charles Beetle, the owner of this business, was an untidy giant with a heart as big and generous as his huge hands — hands with which he was equally skillful in performing feats beyond the strength of others or tasks requiring the delicacy and precision of the lace maker. At first glance, both Charlie and his premises seemed hopelessly messy; but on closer acquaintance one would be very unobservant not to realize that the man had a flair for getting results, while the yard, with its tools and crew, was quickened by the genius of the boss.

The Skipper and Charlie were close friends, and luckily for

me this friendship was broad and deep enough to flow on without a ripple when I was dropped into its current. From being an occasional visitor in company with the Skipper, I gradually became a regular hanger-on at the yard, where without protest I was suffered to poke and pry; until one day Charlie said:

"You've got the hang of this shebang better'n I have — and I guess it's high time you went to work. How about bungin' at a penny apiece?"

"Do you really mean it?" I cried — and on getting a nod in answer, I promptly accepted the proposal.

Early in the morning, as I crossed the fields between The Cottage and "Beetle's" for my first day's work, I was counting the bungs I would drive in hundreds — even in thousands. Aladdin's lamp seemed firmly in hand, and the building shed was magicked to the cave of treasures. I ran the entire way, fearful of losing a profitable moment.

That evening, as I toiled up the rise of those same fields on my way home, every one of the forty bungs I had successfully coped with stood clear in my mind as an impish peg whose sole purpose was to thwart me. No two were exactly the same size; not one would fit on first trial into the countersunk hole for which I chose it; this one split at the first blow of my mallet; that one was cross-grained when I started to chisel it flush with the planking; all of them seemed possessed to jump out of hand — to roll away and hide under the shavings; there was not one but smeared me somewhere when I had dipped it in the pan of white lead and oil. And as if all this were not enough devilment, I found I had to drive most of them lying on my back with the bottom of the boat bearing down on me, so that I ached from cramp, while the fingers of my left hand throbbed from many bruising strokes of my mallet. I would have quit the job there and then had it not been for the thought of Deborah's scornful grin and the Skipper's reproving chuckle. I had to stick it or lose all face.

And so it came about, when a month later, Charlie announced to the gang that he had contracted to build a thirty-one-foot whaleboat and deliver her on a wharf in New Bedford within forty-eight hours, that I, the now recognized "bunger," thrilled at the thought of playing a small part in the race, which would test to the limit the skill and endurance of us all. I took up another hole in my belt and braced myself for the ordeal.

All the whaleboats were constructed in a loft over the main shed. When none of these highly specialized craft were building, this loft was locked, with the key in Charlie's pocket. That hot summer morning when he led five of us up the stairs and through the door, beyond which I had never been, I caught my breath as the orderedness of the place jumped to eye.

The floor — smooth and level as a bowling alley — was free of litter and dust. The parcels of cedar, pine, and oak planking, some cut and shaped, others random length and size, were ranged in neat stacks. There were marked bins with ample stocks of every metal fitting and fastening required. There were molds, battens, clamps, and special tools. There was the steam chest with the pasture-grown white-oak keels, stems, sterns, and rib timbers handy to it. There were knees, apple-wood crotches, loggerheads, rubbing strakes, tholepins, rudders, tillers, mast-steps — all segregated in pigeon holes under the eaves, easy of access. Light and air were streaming in through two rows of skylights in the roof. A line of big oil lamps with reflectors hung from the collar beams overhead. The stage was as carefully set for our play as Henry Irving would have had it; and the actors, but for me, as well drilled.

When I read of the miracles of modern mass production, with emphasis on the newness of the conception of it all, I picture Charles Beetle conducted through an up-to-date shop, with the manager explaining. I can see Charlie's gray eyes twinkle as he listens to the patronizing patter; and, the tour ended, I can hear him pricking his conductor's gassy bubble by mildly suggesting short cuts and shifts that Grandfather Beetle had applied to boat building a hundred years before. The "knocking up" of a whaleboat at Beetle's when I worked there was planned and executed with the exactness and rapidity of an assembly job of today.

Within fifteen minutes after our arrival in the loft Charlie had assigned to every one his job, and I was running downstairs with the drinking-water bucket to fill it at the house well across the road and rush it back to the coolest shadow in the loft, with the coconut dipper laid beside it. At first I thought the work laid out for me was trivial and well within my compass. Before an hour had gone I was sure the success of the whole operation depended on me, and knew it was touch and go whether I could hold up my end. The slap-slapping of the belt lacings on the whirling shaft pulleys was a constant reminder of the ravenous fire under the donkey-engine boiler in the lean-to, where the trash bin, which it was my business to keep full, seemed insatiable. When both the band and buzz saws screeched and the planer yammered, my heart turned over; for I soon learned that these sounds heralded a crisis — the steady decline of boiler pressure — that could be met only by my utmost efforts to find more fuel. I came to hate the ever-desponding needle on the steam gauge; and Charlie's cry of "Water boy!" always rang out at these most feverish moments. The times I refilled that drinking bucket were past all counting.

And just when I felt I had reached the limit of what I could do, came the bleat of a foghorn from Charlie's house — the signal that Mrs. Beetle had the big basket of food and the gallon tin of black coffee ready for me to take to the loft for the first of the half-hour layoffs, recurring thereafter at four-hour intervals.

To sit there on the long bench with the others, swinging my legs to ease the tension out of them, while without speech, with eye and mind vacant, we all munched and swigged, gave me relief and the feeling of having been inducted into the fellowship of artisans — contributing my bit to accomplish a masterpiece — and experiencing for the first time the satisfaction of going all out for a required end. And then, before the delicious sense of relaxation could wear off, Charlie slipped down to the engine, the shafting and pulleys squealed, the belts slapped, and we were all at it again, full bore.

Between ten and eleven o'clock that first night drowsiness stole out of the shadows — first to annoy me and then to become a deadly enemy requiring all my courage and resource to combat. How I stumbled through the hours that followed I cannot tell. I only remember a sense as of reprieve from torture when my upper and lower eyelids came unstuck and my legs and arms seemed once more my own to do with as I chose. And when at last the sizzling lamps were blown out, to fill the loft with the burned-out smell of kerosene and charred wicking, and we all sat again for a spell on the bench, our bloodshot eyes staring at the early light filtering down from above, I shared with the Psalmist the joy that cometh with the morning, after an anxious night.

But, strangely enough, as the hours of the second day passed we all gained rather than lost vigor. As the pace stepped up our reserves of energy seemed to mount, so that when the lamps were lit again and we set ourselves for the last lap, I felt wide awake and fully competent. The final layoff in the light of the last morning turned out to be a lively meal with all hands joshing one another. Our eyes no longer had the look of holes burning in blankets. They were clear, bright, and comprehending as they recurringly came to rest on the graceful boat standing on the floor before us. In her priming coat of gray, she revealed her ancestry. She was the embodiment of Priscilla, the Puritan maiden. We were filled with the pride of parenthood.

By ten o'clock that morning the new boat had been trundled on tupelo rollers to the gaping door in the gable end of the loft and lowered gently and smoothly down the long, well-soaped skid to settle comfortably into the cradle of the "boat gear," with Dobbin, the old bay horse, harnessed into the long shafts. As Charlie, reins in hand, stood in the bow of the boat on the point of clucking Dobbin into motion, his eye caught mine as I stood on the ground below him. Some look on my face must have stirred his ever-generous inclination, for he said:

"Climb aboard, boy, and ride her up to the wharf with me!"

And so, in spite of Dobbin's halting crawl over three long miles, part of it over cobblestones that rattled the teeth in our jaws, the jolting gear became a chariot of victorious warriors to whom a triumph had been granted such as no Roman Caesar ever achieved. So far as I remember we made our progress without words, except that just before we struck the hubbly pavement Charlie observed:

"Give me soft soap enough and a long enough lever and I'd undertake to skid the world from here to breakfast."

Evidently our minds were soaring on the wings of mighty accomplishment.

With an hour to spare before the expiration of the contract, we delivered that boat alongside the *Reindeer,* and waited long enough to see her hoisted on the "cranes," as the davits were called aboard a whaleship. With the mate's receipt for the boat stowed in his pocket, Charlie set about preparing for the journey home. First the sacks of hay that had served as fenders were lashed to the bed timbers of the gear; next, not without protest, I was secured on one of the sacks by several turns of rope around an arm of the cradle; finally Charlie, trussing himself in like fashion, "fished" Dobbin with the reins and we were off. Headed south on Water Street, I found the urge to snooze that Charlie had predicted overcoming me — and, I have no doubt, Charlie, too — for the next sound I recall was the Skipper's voice coming down to me through deeps of sleep, from which I rose sluggishly, to sink again as I slumped, boots and all, onto my bed in The Cottage. After this comes a gap of twenty-four hours in my life of which I have no single memory.

When I showed up at the yard again I found my bunging job had come to an end for the time being, and that I had been shifted from construction to repair, involving me in various operations connected with the marine railway. I liked this new work; for, besides its variety, it gave me an intimate acquaintance with the anatomy, infirmities, and character of all kinds of vessels and their owners, who came to Beetle's as to a surgeon. Many of these clients were fishermen, from whose conversation, highly seasoned as it was, much of interest and value could be gathered. But overtopping all this was my appointment as hostler to old Dobbin, the horse. Hauling the boat gear was for him but an occasional occupation. His principal function was to animate a geared capstan — the power plant of the railway — which deadly monotonous work he had learned to lighten by a turn outrivaling that of any circus clown. Though old and decrepit, Dobbin deserved a gallery of blue ribbons for his acting.

With a boat to be hauled safely blocked and cradled on the inclined rails, I would fetch Dobbin from the lean-to where both he and the donkey engine were stabled. For this work in hand, Dobbin was harnessed with a headstall and single rein, a straw collar and hames, a cotton-webbing saddle and girth, and a pair of long rope traces. As soon as he was in the open the old horse would pause to appraise the heft of the vessel he was about to shift and then pick his way through the gear lying about the yard, to come to a halt finally, tail to a whiffletree hanging from one end of the long horn-timber by which the capstan was revolved. Hooking the traces to the whiffletree and the rein into an eye so placed as to exert a gentle and constant pull on Dobbin's nose to guide him in the arc of the turning horn-timber, I would shout, "Haul ahead!" and on being answered from the cradle-side by "Heave-ho!" I would whack Dobbin on the rump with a frayed wand of whalebone.

The response to this stimulus was pantomime at its best, with Dobbin crouching in a quivering strain, emitting grunts of extreme effort. This pose was followed by a lunge and much scrabbling of hooves, which set the capstan a-turning, the pawls a-clicking and the heavy stud-link chain riding the teeth of the slowly revolving gear.

Keeping one eye cocked on the cradle at the waterside, Dobbin seemed to note the first tremor that ran through the vessel as the pull on the chain started her rolling up the rails — when immediately he would stage a lightning change from the vigorous interest of the willing workman to that of the lazy one disdaining his task. With drooping head, flopping ears and underlip, and vacant eyes, he would shamble round his circular track, worn into a deep furrow, until he reached the point where he must hurdle the chain as it crawled link by link across his course — when suddenly up would jerk his head and forelegs, while with shivering hindquarters he paused for an instant in anticipation of the resounding slap on his flank, delivered by a broad ash lath attached to the horn-timber and automatically raised by a cam until it was released at this critical moment to spur Dobbin to make his jump. From years of practice his reaction to this device had become a classic demonstration of bluff; for the kick of his hind legs and his squeal of anger as he went over the chain said to the thwacker as plainly as words: "Damn you! Wait till I can tear off another lap and kick the stuffin' out of you!"

But by the next step this fiery vigor had evaporated, to be replaced by a feeble scrabble calling for the least possible exertion. Whether the capstan was in high or low gear, making the haul a short or a long operation, Dobbin never varied his act — unless, as sometimes happened, the thwacker broke or slipped off the cam and ceased to function; then Dobbin, too, would quit and stand before the chain, the picture of broken-down machinery. Without the slap of the lath nothing would induce him to jump. It was both annoying and ludicrous to realize that the operation of hauling a boat at Beetle's depended on this mechanical detail — but it was also thundering good advertising, bringing much grist to that mill; for I can remember the ring of enthusiastic fans gathered round the track whenever Dobbin started his performance.

Among the many fishing boats coming frequently to us at Beetle's for repairs was the *Bella*. She was property of her captain who, while he undoubtedly had a legal designation, was known to me always and only as the "Portugee Pirate." I believe he was one of those rare fortunates called an "illiterate" — who are spared the worry and confusion flowing out from the printing press to overwhelm so many of us. As a result, his memory was photographic in its accuracy. His sensory equipment was acute beyond belief. When awake — and I doubt if he ever slept — he vibrated with energy, so that the big earrings that he wore were constantly aquiver. His speech — a seldom dammed torrent — poured out of his great barrel of a chest, a mixture of all the tongues of the Iberian Peninsula, the Western Islands, and the New England waterfront. His single voice in action gave the impression of ten men furiously altercating. To barb his words he brought into play every part of his six-foot-and-over body. Arms, legs, hands, feet, shaggy beard and hair, flashing teeth, and floppy black hat all were called on to impress his hearers that he had the floor and proposed to hold it against all comers.

The *Bella* herself, apple of her owner's eye, was an old, well-built, well-kept, little schooner about sixty feet long. She carried an amazingly big crew of Portuguese, with the consequence that on entering or leaving port she resembled a typhoon in full blast with her master the animating center of the storm. Her ostensible business was the chasing of schooling fish; her less-advertised pursuits smacked of rum and cigars; her decks were sometimes stained with blood from the veins, so it was whispered, of deer and sheep "picked up" on one or another of the Elizabeth Islands. No expense was spared to maintain the *Bella* and her gear in tiptop condition. The year round she came and went on her somewhat mysterious business, and in spite of the tumult and shouting that were a part of her, she successfully evaded both the perils of the sea and those of authority ashore.

There came a soft, foggy day the summer I was bunging when the quiet of the morning was disturbed by a babel of voices from an unseen source behind the gray curtain hiding the harbor. As so often happens, the fog was playing tricks with sound at the time, so that at one moment every word came to us clear and intimate and in the next trailed off to unintelligible murmur. But soon there was enough coherence in what we heard for us to be aware that the riot of sound came from the *Bella,* and that her captain was warning us, and any one else within range, of her approach — and also of the foulness of her bottom; of the rascality of some citizen of Newport who had palmed off on him marine paint that grew rather than de-stroyed vegetation; of vast schools of mackerel lost through this condition; and of the complete destruction which would come to "Sharlie Beedle" and his thrice-condemned yard if the *Bella* were not hauled, scrubbed, painted, and relaunched all within the hours before sunset.

Assured the *Bella* was headed our way, we ran the cradle down the tracks into the water, hitched Dobbin to the capstan, laid out a supply of brooms, buckets, scrapers, and sandpaper, and stood ready to minister to her well-heralded complaints. Suddenly a darker grayness moved in the swaying fog, to sharpen presently into the shape and substance of the familiar little vessel. Another moment and with added tumult she was shot into the eye of the wind, to lower her sails and then glide gently toward the open arms of the cradle. Here, in spite of the captain's fantastic language and action, we soon had the *Bella* blocked and secured, with Dobbin and the thwacker working smoothly. Foot by foot she crawled up the beach out of the sea, and, as the upper strakes of her bottom appeared, her crew were hustled into the water alongside. Immersed to their arm-pits and spurred by their captain's blistering invective, they attacked the slime and weed to such purpose that by the time

86

the *Bella* stood clear on dry land the marine garden had been swept away, and she was prepared for the attentions of the yard gang with their scrapers, sandpaper, brushes, and copper paint.

After stabling Dobbin, there came a few minutes of free time for me, so I climbed aboard the *Bella,* to find her crew very busy mending seine while her master paced the deck impatiently, marking time with reiterated complaints. Walking aft, I looked down the companionway into the cuddy. There the ship's black cat dozed beside the bogie stove, on top of which a pot of beans was simmering. Everything seemed in the usual good order until I came to peer through the port piercing the cabin coaming at an angle that allowed the helmsman a clear view of the compass, always heretofore swung in a box which was screwed to the inner wall of the cabin bulkhead. I was startled to see that this simple but effective binnacle was empty. It was shocking that there should be no compass in sight on so foggy a day. Outraged, I turned to the captain to demand:

"Why, where'd you come from this morning — and where's your compass?"

"Nombre de Dios!" he shouted. "We come from New-*Port* — fog so theek you cut her with knife — compass, Goddam *her,* she meex me all up. I *throw her overboard!*" And with upflung arms he turned away mumbling and moaning, the picture of Job in the midst of his afflictions.

My last sight of the *Bella* and her remarkable owner was on an August night some years after the incident of the compass, when the Skipper and I were sailing to the westward in his yawl *Garland,* close along the northern shore of Naushon Island. As we crossed the mouth of Kettle Cove, with our sails asleep in a gentle and steady southerly breeze, we caught sight of a little schooner anchored deep in the bight. Her foresail, mainsail, and main gaff topsail were standing, her headsails lowered but unfurled — ready for a hurried getaway. Sheered now and then by the offshore puffs, her sails whitened and darkened in the light of a full moon just risen above the hills overhanging the beach. Suddenly downwind from the land's height came a faint shouting, while the silhouette of a man with a load on his back ran across the moon's luminous disk. Six more bowed and hurrying figures appeared and disappeared in rapid succession, to be followed by a seventh who towered above the others, menacing and vocal, leaving no doubt of identity — the Portugee Pirate.

We could only wonder what the loads on these men's backs might be and where they came from; but we had strong suspicion of some little bark or brig, lying perhaps at that very moment in Tarpaulin Cove across the Island, having arrived the afternoon before from the West Indies. And so, in an atmosphere of mystery and romance, the *Bella* and her crew slide from my further knowledge and vision, just as they disappeared on the summer night when the westerly horn of Kettle Cove hid them from us as we stole silently on our way.

SEVEN

Journey Cakes

EARLY ONE April, I joined the Skipper on board his cruising boat *Garland* at Norfolk, Virginia. I found the Old Man short-tempered, with impatience to be off and away on the voyage home to New Bedford, where he had agreed to deliver me on a certain day; for I was in my last year at school, and Easter vacations had a way of ending abruptly on specified dates.

The *Garland* was a fifty-foot yawl. She had been built for the Skipper the summer before at Beetle's Boat Yard on Clark's Point. Fife, of Fairlie, Scotland, had designed her. She was flush-decked and the rig was snug; but I thought her too heavy a vessel to be handled by so small and light a crew as ours. The Skipper's gray hairs put him in the "venerable" class; and Willie Lucas, a young neighbor of ours on the Point, was no more of a seasoned sailor than I was.

However, by the time we were abreast of Montauk Point, I had the feeling that Willie and I, not counting the Skipper, could "handle the sticks out of her," for we had made a wonderful run of it so far, with a steady south-southwest wind, clear, warm days and nights, a smooth sea, and regular hot meals.

Fourteen hours later my confidence had disappeared; so, too, had the serving of regular hot meals. Our good breeze having deserted us in the late afternoon, a dead calm had kept us rolling and wallowing through the early hours of the night; and then, at about eight bells, a strong northeast wind had made its boisterous appearance. Since then we had been beating to windward under reefed sails, and had had to face, without letup, an incessant bombardment of heavy spray and a sniping of snow, hail, and rain that came screaming at us in thin showers from the cover of a low, gray, hurrying sky.

This combined attack had worked through our defense of oilskins, sou'westers, towels around our necks, and sea boots, until we were lumps of icy pulp, longing to exchange the hammer and splash, the procession of white-crested, steely seas, and the cold, searching wind for the quiet of an anchorage.

By midafternoon the wind backed two points and blew harder. It was clear that we could not fetch New Bedford by daylight; but we could lay up through Vineyard Sound on the port tack with a fair tide and smooth water under the lee of the Elizabeth Islands. By this change in course we were able, as dusk was coming on, after a lively beat through the tide-tortured gut of Woods Hole, to ease sheets and commence twisting our way into the land-locked haven of Hadley Harbor, Naushon Island. Both Willie and I shivered with relief when we felt the wind on our backs instead of in our faces — but the Skipper, in spite of his gray hairs, sat there on the steering bench with the long tiller tucked under his left arm and gave no outward sign of his emotions. As we made the last turn and opened the inner pool to sight, all hedged about with wind-clipped oaks and beeches, there lay the old *Myra,* beamy and comfortable — a very homey sight.

Before anchoring the *Garland,* the Skipper steered close under the *Myra*'s stern and hailed her. Instantly the slide of her companion was shoved forward and a head with silvery hair was inquiringly poked out.

"I'll match a bottle of my Braganza against one of your dinners if you'll come aboard us and cook it, Captain Wasque," barked the Skipper, as we rounded up into the eye of the wind and slowly forged ahead, with the mainsail and the sheet blocks slatting and banging.

Up went the Captain's right arm with that sweeping gesture of acceptance — the universal and perhaps oldest signal in the code of the sea. And, twenty minutes later, when the *Garland* had settled into her berth with sails furled and stopped, ropes coiled, and riding light set for the night, Captain Wasque and his inseparable mate, Theoph Crowell, came alongside in their skiff. Spurred by a fierce shower of hail that rattled down on us at this moment, they boarded the *Garland* in a hurry, after handing up to us a basket that crackled and quaked with a constant weaving motion, and with it a fetch bag, bulging with sundries that evidently called for protection from the wet.

No one of average build, standing beside Captain Wasque for the first time, could fail to feel both gross and clumsy. His delicacy suggested a porcelain figurine, perfect in proportions and of fragile workmanship. Seventy years and the sun and wind of the Seven Seas had not tanned the pink out of his cheeks, nor creased his face and neck with lines. Everything about him was fitting and very clean, and, although he wore on his tiny feet a pair of women's black, glazed-kid, buttoned boots — scallops and all — this rather startling finishing touch was so in scale with the rest of him that it did not strike a false note.

Shaking hands with the Skipper and running his eye over the *Garland*'s deck and gear, the Captain turned and disappeared down the companionway like a chipmunk diving into a stone wall and was followed by his ponderous Man Friday with the bag and basket.

Much as we longed to be below with our friends in the shelter and warmth of the cabin, the Skipper, Willie, and I had to spend ten disagreeable minutes more on that wet, hail-swept deck while we fumbled over buttons with numb, wizened fingers in our struggle to peel off the outer layers of our sodden clothing.

The dinghy that lay bottom up over the skylight made a shelter for these discarded wrappings; and there, as soon as possible, we left them and slithered down the companion ladder in our stocking feet, singlets, and drawers.

Theoph, the Good Samaritan, as we landed on the cabin floor, handed us three heavy-bottomed bar glasses which he had filled with a pale liquor that had a white bead on top. "Sup that up slow," said he, as he dusted the bead with powdered cinnamon from a salt shaker.

As the first "sup" reached my vitals I felt the stirring of hope, and by the time I had swallowed the whole of my drink this sprout had grown to a vigorous plant with tendrils reaching out to my frozen extremities.

"What is it?" I asked.

"Bridgetown snorter," replied Theoph. "Barbados XXX rum, lime juice, Falernum, a dash of angostura, white of an egg beaten stiff, a lump of ice, and a hell of a stir — smooth, ain't it?"

"You bet!" thought I, as, following the Skipper's example, I stood naked and glowing after a rubdown with a coarse crash towel.

Meantime Captain Wasque, swathed in a white apron, hovered busily over the coal-burning cook stove that now, purring fiercely, was filling the cabin with warmth and teasing our craving for food with savory odors.

Turning to the Captain, the Skipper, dry, clothed, and pleasantly relaxed, asked an old man's unvarying question after an absence from home: "Who died since I've been away?"

"Nobody *much,*" was the reply. "Only Wash Peck over to Central Village, my Myry's first cousin, the fella that was always runnin' rum or cigars or liftin' sheep or cows — you remember him. I *had* to go to his funeral. Lot of folks there — interested to see the end of him, I guess. Fella from away presided at the meetin'; said he: 'I've been ex*horted* an' im*portuned* to preach Brother Peck's funeral sermon, 'n' I don't want to. He was a bad man an' you all know it. He kep' hosses an' he rin 'em; he kep' cocks an' he fit 'em; but they do say he was *occasionarily* good to a fire. We will now all jine in singin' hymn one hundred: "With rapture we rejice the cuss [curse] is now removed." ' Kinder short, wan't it? But most folks seemed real pleased — an' now, boys, come an' get it!'"

The dinner Captain Wasque dished up for us that night was surely a thing of beauty. As he stood at the after end of the table dealing out the piping-hot willow-pattern Canton plates, his apron and silvery hair seemed to imbue him with priestly authority. He proceeded, as if performing a ritual, to put a clean, folded dishclout in the middle of the table, on which he set a blue bowl of snow-white mashed potato that had been whipped to a creamy smoothness and mossed lightly with the green of chopped chives. Next to this, hot from the oven, he placed a brown earthenware baking dish capped with a golden crust of bread and cracker crumbs that had been worked into a paste with butter flavored with a few drops of lemon juice. Under this crust, which heaved slightly from internal pressure, there lay, as we presently discovered, the tenderest parts of the eight live lobsters that had come aboard in the crackling basket, together with morsels of the green fat. As a catalyst in this compound the Captain had used a thin white sauce flavored with two tablespoonfuls of "Bristol Milk"; and as a sign of his deep friendship for us he lastly presented a pan of what he called "Rye Injun Journey Cakes" — the recipe for which no one could ever wring from him.

As we were about to dip into these good things, all sizzling hot, an unusually heavy squall swept singing through the *Garland*'s rigging, to be followed immediately by the annoying slap-slap-slap of a slack halyard against the mainmast. "Whose slippery hitch is that?" said the Skipper, eyeing me with reproof. "Mine, I guess," I had to answer, as I squeezed by Willie to go on deck.

It was cold, wet, and dark up there, and I did not linger. Hurrying back through the forehatch, I slipped on my wet soles, so that I came below on the run, fetching up in the forecastle with a crash and reaching my place at table shaken, subdued, and moist.

As I suppose time is reckoned, it was only a scant half hour before the blue bowl and the brown baking dish stood there on their white mat as cleanly empty as the day they were drawn from the kiln. The journey cakes had gone too; for they had a crispness and a flavor suggestive of salted almonds right out of the oven, so that we were continually helping ourselves to "just one more."

And now the Skipper, faithful to his promise, brought from the spirit locker five slender-stemmed glasses enriched with delicate designs in gold leaf, and also a quart bottle of so dark a green that, as it stood on the table jinking in the light of the slightly swaying lamp, it glowed a jet black. Against this background the crude white letters and figures painted on the irregularly rounded sides were thrown into high relief. To the initiated, these marks on the girth of the bottle and the cap of red wax on the long neck were guarantees that the contents were a portion of those two pipes of Madeira that had been laid down in New Bedford years ago after a three-year whaling voyage in the ship *Braganza*.

As the Captain set his second pan of cakes on the table, the Skipper, using great care, cracked the seal and drew the cork of that bottle, while Willie and I cleared away the plates and silver.

"I propose the toast, 'To absent friends,' " said the Skipper, after he had charged the glasses and passed his own under his nose and held it to the light; and I can remember that as the first sip lacquered my tongue and trickled down my throat the last shred of the discomfort of the preceding twenty-four hours faded away and was replaced by the exaltation of accomplishment — the job well done.

The passage of time and sequence of happenings for that evening now come to an end for me. I only know that as the hard squalls buffeted the *Garland,* causing her to shift her head and quiver as her masts and rigging vibrated, I had a sense of security never experienced on shore; and that the bronze green of the floor planking, the Chinese red of the sheathing, the white of the deck planking overhead, and the occasional roar of the burnished copper stovepipe all combined to make of that little cabin a palace of contentment and delights — where I could lie full stretch on the transom cushion listening to the low-pitched conversation of the three old men and watching the blue smoke of their cigars drifting and eddying about, to soften all angles and to perfume as with an incense.

At last I heard the Skipper, who had been nibbling a journey cake between the regular circulations of the Braganza, say with emphasis: "Captain Wasque, you know you're living now on borrowed time. I think it's your duty to give me a written record of how you concoct these cakes of yours. Now come across — clean!"

"Oh, gammon!" said the Captain, with a grin of satisfaction. "This harbor here and Bub's fall tonight puts me in mind of the old *Euphrates,* Cap'n John Smith, that was owned by Fish an' Grinnell of Noo York. The Hillman Brothers built her in New Bedford — oak for her timbers was cut right here on Naushon. They run her as a packet between Noo York an' Havre. Cap'n Smith, the mate Elihu Jones, an' th' second mate Hosea Robinson, was all drivers — out to make records for the ship 'n' 'emselves — no liquor while at sea — but Mister Jones when in port used to bowse his jib up pretty taut once'n a while.

"One mornin' when they was dischargin' cargo an' had the main hold cleared with the main hatch wide open, Mister Jones, who'd been ashore, come flyin' on board an' started across-deck to bawl out one o' the hands he thought was sojerin'; but, not lookin' where his feet was goin', he stubbed his toe on the main hatch coamin' an' pitched head fust into the hold. Cap'n Smith was on the quarterdeck, an' believin' there'd been a fatal accident, he sings out to the second mate: 'Mister Robinson, take two hands and the fall of a whip an' bring Mister Jones's body on deck!'

"All who'd seen that dive was sure the mate was a corpse, for the drop was considerable an' the keelson a hard landin' place. Down the ladder to the 'tween decks went the second mate an' the two hands an' disappeared into the dark o' the hold. For a while nothin' happened — then up come Mister Robinson an' the hands again, lookin' kinder sheepish; but no signs o' the mate.

" 'Mister Robinson,' says the Cap'n, 'what about Mister Jones, an' why did you leave him below instead o' bringin' his body on deck as I ordered?'

"Before the second mate could answer, Mister Jones himself, lookin' very cross an' marked up considerable, comes bouncin' out o' the hatch, runs up to the second mate, an' wagglin' his fist in his face, bawls out: 'Can't I go down below on this ship, *when* I want to, *the way* I want to, without you follerin' me around?'

"An' that," ended Captain Wasque, "is the way I feel about them Rye Injun Journey Cakes."

EIGHT

Match Race

O
N A DAY early in August a letter from the Skipper came to me at the office in Boston where I was then employed. Inasmuch as it was a command to join him aboard his yawl *Garland* on Friday evening, August 24th, "without fail," I suspected him of planning a trip more adventurous than a weekend cruise.

Braced by the possibilities of what might be in the wind, I faced up to my boss and asked for leave of absence on Saturday, the 25th. With great emphasis on the favor extended, my prayer was grudgingly granted, and I slugged through the intervening days with what patience I could muster, until at last I hailed the *Garland* from the wharf-end in Padanaram Harbor late in the evening of the appointed day. Lord! How fresh and cool, after sweltering days in town, the salty air smelled and tasted as Willie Lucas rowed me out! And when I'd pitched my bundle of oilskins, boots, and sweater on deck and jumped aboard after it, I felt I stood there cleansed of the grime of commerce.

"Regular — job of work — on our hands — tomorrow — match race — schooner *Belle* — one thousand — dollars a side!" Willie had grunted between strokes on our way out, fanning my anticipation to feverishness, so that I did not linger on deck but hurried below to get the lowdown from the Skipper.

"Come aboard, come aboard — and glad to see you!" said he, as I landed at the foot of the companion ladder to stand blinking in the light of the lamp hanging under the skylight.

"You know Theoph Crowell; and this" — motioning toward a stranger, very spruce in braided, brass-buttoned Yacht Club uniform — "is Captain Van Courtland, who's kindly joined us as observer — for we've matched the *Garland* to beat the *Belle,* boat for boat, tomorrow; fair or foul weather and no cutting of corners."

The nod in return for my bow to this newcomer across the table was chilling — somehow patronizing. Instinctively I dubbed him "Dry Goods Commission Agent" — a designation commonly applied to the new generation of traders in New York by the old-time ship owners and merchants, which carried with it the reproach of "play-acting" — not quite the real thing — particularly when it involved would-be sailor men. There was a sense of satisfaction in so settling the status of our guest, and, as I slid myself into a seat on the narrow transom cushion beside the warm, friendly bulk of old Theoph, I felt comfortably a part of both ship and crew.

"Two gun flyin' start, 9:00 A.M. — on line between mark boat and White Rock," whispered Theoph, shoving toward me a chart spread on the table, "and thence to Sow and Pigs reef — with lightship to port — out to Noman's, South West Buoy mark to starboard — and from there around Block Island, north- or south-about, optional — and return to start, leavin' Hen and Chickens lightship on port hand," he continued, tracing the course with his tholepin of a forefinger. "Give a feller gray hairs figurin' tides and weather, or I'm a Jonah! Wasque, he joins early tomorrer, so, thank God, we'll have hot vittles, blow high or low!"

Picking up the dividers, I pricked off the distance between the marks, to be impressed by the total, rising one hundred sea miles — while Theoph, muffling his voice to an even lower key, carried on with further details of the match:

" 'S far's I can figure, last month — down to Noo York — the Skipper was to one o' them high-toned Yacht Club dinners; and after they'd eat and drunk considerable, this Cap'n Bleeker that owns the *Belle* says he'd heard how the Skipper'd deserted the American centerboarder and got himself married to a British-designed and rigged deep-keeler.

"Well, after that it wan't long before all hands had took sides and was at it hammer and tongs — cutter versus schooner — resultin' at last in the Skipper's layin' he'd got fifty-six foot of plank and fastenin's — *and a lead keel* — he'd match to beat any centerboard schooner up to sixty-five foot they was willin' to risk on an outside course, not less'n a hundred miles."

As I grasped the implications of this undertaking, my pleasurable excitement cooled to soberness. The stakes bulked, while our chances of winning dwindled. I stole a glance at the Skipper, who stood to lose what seemed to me a fortune, and was momentarily cheered by hearing him laugh as he talked with his guest. And then, looking at the clock, he said to me:

"Time to turn in, old man. You'll bunk forward with Willie, and turn out at five to make up light sails and fetch Cap'n Wasque aboard at six, so's to have breakfast at seven sharp."

Sidling forward between the table and starboard transom, with a "Good night, all!" I passed from the light of the cabin into the darkness of the forecastle. Here, after a little fumbling, I found and loosed the lanyard securing the port-side folding berth, shed my shoes and jacket, and stretched myself on the thin mattress, to lie wide awake for a long time, listening to Willie's even breathing coming from the opposite berth, the occasional lapping of ripples against the bow planking, and the whisperings of the breeze in the rigging, while my mind whirled with the problems and possibilities of the coming day. It was irritating to realize that life ashore was getting the better of my former ability to drop asleep instantly when afloat. "Hang it all," I thought, "I'm getting old, with habit clamping me down into a groove!" And suddenly here was Willie bending over me and twitching my left foot, while the light of a gray morning streamed down through the half-opened forehatch. And a minute later I'd followed him up the ladder to the deck.

One look 'round at the weather was enough to proclaim that the day was to be unfavorable to us. Already at this early hour the southwest wind was coming in strong puffs — harbingers of more to follow — with the probability of a thunder squall in the afternoon; conditions giving our big antagonist a great advantage.

And there she lay out beyond us, as sleek as patent leather, her varnished spars looming tall through the wisps of fog blowing by and packing to leeward in an ever-thickening cloud, the color of lead, under which the ruffled surface of the Bay assumed an ominous green. I felt we were David confronting Goliath, and hoped the Skipper might prove a potent pebble.

But at this moment the Old Man himself popped up from below, to lift the grating from a hatchway aft of the companion coaming and drop down into the sail room. A minute later he was lighting up to Willie and me, one after the other, the balloon, number 1, number 2, and baby jib topsails, and last the thimble-headed gaff topsail.

"Single-reefed mainsail with topsail over it I guess'll be the style today," said he as he climbed on deck again, to hand us a couple of hanks of light sail twine cut into varying lengths. "And get a move on stopping those headsails — and God help you if any of 'em don't break out when the time comes," he continued, as he lugged the gaff topsail forward to the foot of the main mast.

So adjured, Willie on the port side and I on the starboard, set to work making up those seemingly endless yards of cloth, which continually crawled and ballooned as, kneeling over them, we folded, patted, stretched, and finally stopped them into long, neat tapers. How we cursed the wind, the sails, and the lengths of twine, blown out of our fingers even after the Skipper joined us to lend a hand. It was a pernickety job under the conditions, from which I was thankful to be relieved when ordered into the dinghy to go ashore for Cap'n Wasque, whom I found waiting on the wharf, neat and dapper as ever, with his familiar fetch bag in hand, and accompanied by Nils, a huge Swede.

"Weather looked kinder bilious this mornin' — figured Nils'd come in handy later — so I fetched him along," remarked the Captain as he lowered himself into the stern sheets, while I jammed myself into the bows after turning the oars over to Nils.

"I ban good man when she blows," volunteered Nils as he made that dinghy fairly jump through the harbor chop. "You bet!" thought I, as I pictured him laying onto that mainsheet when we came to the turn at Noman's buoy.

As we shot alongside the *Garland,* the Skipper stood at the rail to greet us cheerfully with:

"Bully for you, Captain! We can use all that beef on the hoof you've brought along today — and whatever's in your bag, too," and reaching down to the little old man handed him on deck in a hurry.

"Topside-up or down — I'll cook!" said the Captain, diving below, while Nils, Willie, and I hoisted the dinghy aboard and lashed her, bottom up, over the already battened-down skylight. "Just so there won't be any deserters before we start," chuckled the Skipper as he leaned over to tie the last knot.

At this moment old Theoph hove himself out of the companion with a steaming coffeepot in one hand and tin mugs in the other, to announce: "Come all ye faithful, turn from labor to refreshment — for it's a long pull yet to breakfast," and rang-ing the cups on the steering bench he filled them and commenced to loose the ties of the sail covers.

With a mugful of the well-sweetened coffee stowed away, it was surprising to find the looks of the weather improved in spite of the thickening sky and strengthening wind. And, in my own case, it was encouraging to realize the odds on the race were more even, as we fell to work again tucking a reef into the mainsail, bending the small, thimble-headed jigger, bowsing home the bobstay tackle, hauling out and hoisting the number 2 jib in stops, and making countless other preparations for getting underway. So many willing, experienced hands, and Theoph's frequent gibes, lightened the work and made it go with a bounce. And, by the time Cap'n Wasque had raised a devilish racket with an iron spoon and frying pan calling us to breakfast, the *Garland* was ready to hoist sail and be off.

Squeezed tightly around the table, with our coffee mugs refilled, and devouring beefsteaks, cottage-fried potatoes, and corn bread, we were a silent but industrious crew. Nils, however, enlivened the meal by certain smacking and supping sounds evidencing his willingness to share his enjoyment. Glancing at our "observer," I thought his nose was steeved at an even sharper angle than it had been last evening. And when Cap'n Wasque remarked, "Beef's the ballast that don't fetch loose in a seaway," our guest showed signs that he felt out of place in this company, and lit a Corona as we swabbed up the gravy on our plates with the last of the corn bread.

"And now, Commodore," said the Skipper, addressing Captain Van Courtland, "if you'll excuse us we'll leave you to finish your smoke in peace, while we get sail on her" — and as he passed me on his way to the ladder he whispered: "You stay here below and help old Wasque with the stowage."

By the time the spry little Captain and I had everything shipshape, including a big kettle of beef stew clamped on the stove to simmer, I heard the Skipper sing out from aft: "All clear!" — which was followed by a stir of feet, a shifting of ropes, a tremor, and then an ever-increasing inclination of the port side, the crisp slap of a wavelet on the starboard bow, and the unmistakable forward thrust as the *Garland* gathered headway. Jumping for the ladder, I climbed on deck just as the foresail rose slatting up the stay, to quiet down presently as Theoph and I sweated in and belayed the sheet.

When the staysail ceased its flogging, the Skipper, upping the helm a trifle, gave the *Garland* a hard full. Off from the shore came a strong puff of wind and down went our lee rail into a lather of streaming foam, swirls of which spilled inboard, darkening the white deck.

"And now she moves!" rumbled Theoph, as he and I crawled up to windward, while the *Garland* rapidly closed the distance between us and the still-anchored *Belle*. In a rush we passed close along her weather side as her big crew tailed onto her main halyards, while our Skipper, lifting his cap, waved it in salutation to a ruddy-faced gentleman standing aft near her wheel. As this civility was acknowledged, Captain Van Courtland, who had come from below, stretched out his arms and pointedly, as it seemed to me, shook hands with himself.

Out in the Bay we found all the wind we wanted for our snug rig; and as we came abreast of White Rock — the weather end of the starting line — the *Garland* began to dust her foredeck with spray as she hit the chop kicked up by the current of the hour-old ebb. A half-mile farther to the south below an ever-thickening curtain of fog we could dimly see the whitecaps of steep seas jostling in the narrow pass between Sandspit shoal and Dumpling Rock, where the foghorn blared forlornly.

"Ready about!" called the Skipper, easing the long tiller to leeward, "and hand that staysail while she's in the wind."

Up came the *Garland*'s bow in a long sweep to windward; down fluttered the staysail into Nils's smothering arms, while he ducked his head like a boxer to avoid the blocks on the jib-sheet pennants, lashing out as the jib traversed over the forestay to be sheeted down by Theoph and me, while Willie and

Cap'n Wasque, who had nipped on deck to lend a hand, set up the port-side runner tackle. Farther and farther swung the bow until, with the wind on her quarter and sheets flattened in, we were running slowly back for the starting line which had now been established by Captain Bill West in his old sloop *Theresa,* anchored two cable lengths ENE of White Rock. A few minutes later we were running close along the *Theresa*'s port side and Cap'n Wasque was standing at our weather rail, his watch in hand, ready to take the time.

"Eight — forty-two — fifty!" hailed Captain Bill, his eyes on his own watch, and "Eight — forty-two — fifty!" echoed old Wasque, adjusting his timepiece as we slid past the *Theresa*'s stern and hauled our wind to make way for the *Belle,* coming up from to leeward, her four lowers unreefed, as flat as boards.

"Stands up to it like a church," commented the Skipper, eyeing our rival, "— and sails like a witch," he added enthusiastically, as the sleek black hull knifed through the chop to range alongside the *Theresa,* with sails lifting to kill her headway as she, too, checked on the time.

"That whole mainsail o' hern worries the Skipper considerable — I don't think," said Theoph to me with a grin, as the *Garland* lay down to a savage puff and stretched away to the northwest.

Nine minutes later, after threading our way through a patch of foul ground which the *Belle* — a stranger — was bound to steer clear of, we wore the *Garland* round and headed back for White Rock sharp on the wind and on the starboard tack. Three long minutes passed in silence. "And there she talks!" barked Cap'n Wasque, as a burst of smoke clouded the *Theresa,* to be followed in a few seconds by the cannon's thud.

That report, like the twist of a fiddle key, tautened our nerves. With but five minutes to cover it, the stretch ahead to the Rock looked long, while, off to leeward through the murk loomed the *Belle,* heading for the line on the port tack.

"Four!" chirped our timekeeper, and we shifted uneasily, all eyes outboard to measure the dwindling distance, and again inboard to watch the Skipper's face for a sign. A breathless pause of half a minute, and then it came: "Give her the staysail!" which sent Willie and Nils forward on the run and Theoph and me scrambling to leeward to tend sheet. "And three to go!" shrilled Wasque, as the *Garland* leaped to the lift of the added sail.

From where I squatted on the lee deck, hanging onto a cleat for support, my outlook was narrowed to the scene to leeward where the *Belle* held the center of the stage. "By the Lord! How she comes on!" I thought. "And can she nip by ahead of us to tack on our weather bow and have us beat before we're started — or can we squeeze by her nose, leaving her to come about in our wake and take our dust?"

In that question was crammed the fate of the world, which minutes — seconds now — would resolve.

My mouth felt full of cotton wool; I couldn't even swallow. "And two to go!" came faintly through to my consciousness, as the *Belle* pressed on, faster and faster, while the poor old *Garland* seemed to slug along, painfully slow.

And now the question itself narrowed to: She has us — no, not yet — she has — she *hasn't*. An eternity of held breath — a sound as of swishing silk from the *Belle* tearing through the water — and suddenly, with room to spare, we shot across her bow!

"Eureka! That's a relief," grunted Theoph beside me, as, freed from the menacing thrust of the *Belle*'s long bowsprit, we rapidly opened her weather side to view.

"And one!" chanted Wasque, commencing to tick off the remaining seconds — "One — two — three" while the tension built up again at the thought that we might reach the line ahead of the gun. "Twenty-five — twenty-six" — how slowly those seconds ran, and how fast the *Garland* ate up the distance still to go! "Damn it all! Suppose we have to run her off to leeward down that line, waiting for that infernal cannon, while the *Belle*

— a few seconds astern — comes up to rob us of our well-earned pride of place!" The thought was too much for me, and I crawled to windward to have a look ahead.

"Forty-two — forty-three — forty-four" — sixteen more seconds; and we were nearly abreast of the north nubbin of White Rock. "Oh, what's the use," I thought, "the fat's already in the fire!"

And at that instant, as a hard puff struck ahead, the Skipper gave the *Garland* a sharp sheer to windward, damping her headway — and when the squall eased he wound her off, just clear of the steep-to rock. "And sixty!" came the count; and then "Whang!" the report of the gun; with yards still to go before we cut the line, going great guns and a rapful.

At the Skipper's command to "freshen the nips on all halyards!" I crawled aft to set up the jig of the mizzen, and passing our observer on the way, gave him a look which I hoped he'd interpret as, "How's that for a start, Mister Corona Corona? — and be damned to yuh!" But getting no change for my pains, I took it out on the tackle until the luff of the sail stood taut as the head of a drum.

Jamming the last turn of the fall on the pin, I looked astern at the *Belle* lying down to it in our wake. "No use teasing myself watching her," I thought, starting to crawl forward again to join the others prone along the weather rail. Presently the *Garland* knocked into a little sea and a shower of spray slashed aboard. "Oilskins and sou'westers — two at a time," ordered the Skipper, sending us below in couples to get into our crackling armor.

At the head of the ladder on my way back to the deck I took another squint at our competitor. Either we'd eaten out to windward or she was being sailed wide; for she was no longer in our wake, but had crept up on our lee quarter. As I started for my station the Skipper beckoned and I slithered over the wet deck to his side. In a low voice he said: "I'm pinching her to go through the pass to windward of Sandspit buoy — the fog'll shut down thick by the time we're through the rip. Pass the word we'll tack while they can still see us aboard the *Belle* — and fetch my waterproof and the Commodore's, too."

Coming up from the companionway, I was erupted, my arms full of oilskins, and thrown sprawling — a most unseamanlike evolution — at the Skipper's side by a sharp scend of the *Garland* when, picked up and tossed by the first of the confused, leaping seas, she plunged into the rip. Again I felt the coldness of the Van Courtland eye as I handed over his long coat and sou'wester. For five minutes 'twas a case of "hold on all," while we were swept through the pass, jouncing, jolting, and baptized by driving sprays, to shoot out finally into the less-disturbed seas beyond the bell buoy.

A look to leeward, and there, dimly, was the *Belle,* now broad on our beam and sailing fast. A look ahead and to windward: nothing but opaque grayness, confining the vision to a few yards, with here and there the white head of a sea gleaming palely.

"Ready about!" ordered the Skipper, sending us to our stations; and then "Hard-a-lee!" came the call, followed by a momentary confusion of slatting sails, banging blocks, and whirring sheaves, as the *Garland* righted to an even keel, poised for an instant on the crest of a sea, and, as the sails filled, dipped her starboard rail and was off on the port tack, heading into the smother.

A minute or two passed, while I watched the *Belle* cross our wake and grow fainter and fainter as we diverged from her course. "Is she going to stay on the starboard tack and split with us?" I wondered; and just as I concluded, "Yes, she is," her bow, riding up on a sea, turned toward us, her sails fluttered, then hardened — and there she was, after us again, but to windward of our wake. A minute more, and the fog blotted her out, and at that instant the *Garland* was tacked again, and I was called to relieve the Skipper at the helm.

As I settled down on the bench to take over from him he whispered: "Foxed 'em that time, I think. Sail her fine and let that lee-bow tide soak her out to windward — and watch the wind, it's inclined to haul."

My first five minutes at the helm were of sweating intensity — one half of me concentrated on getting the feel of her and keeping her going on the thin edge of the squally wind, and one half trying to catch sight or sound of the *Belle* crossing our course ahead or astern, or tacking to windward or to leeward of us. But finally it was evident we'd missed her and would have to content ourselves with the uncertainty of whether or not we'd teased her into a long port tack, as the Skipper had hoped to do. For profit or loss, we ourselves were now committed to a long starboard board, and I settled down to steer with everything I had to give.

For the best part of an hour the only sounds and stir aboard the *Garland* were of her own making — the rhythmic swash of her lee-bow wave, the sudden volleys of spray hard driven on deck and sails, the gentle but constant hiss of the sudsy stream running swiftly along her lee rail, the shrilling of the wind, now high, now low, in her bar-taut rigging, the clack of a block, the creak of a strop, and the general plouter of bruised water, as she shouldered through an ever-rougher sea and deepening gloom on her course across the mouth of the Bay.

Enveloped and blinded as we were by clouds of swirling vapor, the whoop at three-minute intervals of the Dumpling Rock foghorn had been for a while our only link with a fixed world. But no sooner had we come to depend on this tie, than — "Phut!" — it had been cut off by some trick of unstable air currents, leaving us to sail on alone in a cramped, dim sphere.

At the time I'd taken over the helm Willie had brought our Lathrop patent horn on deck and had raised his hand to pump out a blast, when the Skipper had sung out:

"Go easy on that music box for a while. Steve Brodie took a chance, and so'll we 'til something moves our way. No good advertising more'n we have to, just now." And then, after a look at the compass, he'd gone below to work a traverse with his watch, dividers, parallel rule, and chart. Five minutes later he was beside me again, checking my performance, the trim of the sails, our course by compass, and the variations in both direction and weight of the breeze. For a good half-hour he continued these comings and goings between deck and chart table, during which time the wind had gradually shifted clockwise until the *Garland* was heading into the blinding fog a trifle west, instead of a trifle east, of south.

Then, startlingly, without warning, from off to windward came the thuttering moan of the horn on Hen and Chickens lightship, answered a moment later by a fainter growl from Sow and Pigs, broken into from astern by the now faraway hoot of Dumpling Rock; while at the same time the seas shortened and sharpened, as, laying down to it in a squall, we drove into another tide rip.

As if summoned by the horns, the fog closed in on us thicker than ever, until our thrusting bowsprit seemed to be ripping its way into folds of a dark curtain; and I'd just muttered, "This beats Steve Brodie and the chance *he* took," when the pall over the truck on our sharply inclined topmast thinned and blew apart, to expose a rounded hilltop suspended miraculously in the sky to leeward. One more stab of the bowsprit, and the curtain had split from the rent overhead to its hem that swept the water, leaving an ever-expanding view of grassy uplands, rocky foreshore, a white beach, and Cuttyhunk lighthouse ahead of us, fine on our weather bow.

"And now," said the Skipper to me, "I'll take her again. And pass the word to Cap'n Wasque that as soon as we've tacked the sun'll be over the yardarm."

Shoved bodily to windward by the strong ebb current pouring out of Pune — the passage between Cuttyhunk and Penikese islands — we made top speed into the "smooth" under the lee of Sow and Pigs reef, to tack presently abreast of the lighthouse and stand out to the northwest. As the *Garland* settled into her stride on her new course, Cap'n Wasque appeared at the head of the companion ladder with a bottle of Barbados rum in one hand and a tin mug in the other. Wedging himself between the slide and the fashion-board, he crowed, "All hands to splice the main brace!" And as there was a general move toward him, he warned, "One at a time, and no crowding!"

"Come, Commodore — you lead off," said the Skipper to our guest, who had been strangely silent and inert throughout the morning, but who now, so admonished, hitched himself gingerly across the deck to swallow his tot and crawl back to his post at the foot of the jigger mast. One by one the rest of us followed him; until, when my turn had come, and after the mellow fire had reached my vitals and extremities, I found myself humming: "We'll rant and we'll roar like true British sailors, etc.," as I chammed a pantile of hard ship's bread, one of which had been passed out with each drink. This warm confidence held us, in spite of our having run out of the clear hole over Cuttyhunk into cold, wet fog as thick or thicker than it had been before.

A half hour followed during which, in a seaway growing uncomfortably rougher, we tacked three times, while the "grauuuch" of the horn on Sow and Pigs lightship played hide and seek with us in the fog. And when for a fourth time we'd lost all trace of it, Theoph voiced our feelings by grumbling, "God damn it! I'll bet those hayseeds have quit blowin' and gone below to dinner, just when we thought we'd nailed 'em on a firm bearin'."

But still the minutes passed without a sign while all hands grew irritably tense from straining ears and eyes; until, just as a green sea boarded us to fill the deck, rail high, Willie, his mouth as usual full of tobacco, mumbled something and pointed forward, where as if by magic a dense black wall of fog resolved itself into the big red hull of the pitching lightship, right ahead and very near. A sudden yaw to starboard, a dive into another sea, and we drove by her to windward, close enough for two

110

faces gaping at us over her rail to show pink under their glistening black sou'westers, while a cloud of steam, feathering out from her chime whistle, blew to leeward without a sound's reaching us.

Stupefied for a moment by the eeriness of this apparition, which faded out as quickly as it had come, we were brought back to reality by the order: "Stand by to ease sheets!" and by the sudden blare of the horn as we broke out of its unaccountably mute sector. Then slowly and with care, for the seas here in the mouth of the Sound were steep and high and the breeze hardening, the *Garland* was steered onto her course for the Noman's buoy. The sails were trimmed for a close reach, and Willie told off at last to show his skill on our "music box."

Up to this time, thanks to the Skipper's intimate knowledge of local conditions, the wind and tide and even the fog had all lent us a hand on our way. But now we had to face a stretch of twelve miles of open sea, disturbed by tidal currents of varying strength and direction, at the end of which was a lone buoy — four miles south of Noman's Land, the nearest fixed point — that we must sight and leave to starboard before hauling onto the wind again to commence our forty-mile beat to Block Island. In so dense a fog, and the now heavy sea, to pick up that mark, even though it was an automatic "whistler," posed the old problem of the needle in the haystack — which, regardless of careful steering and pilotage, might cause so much fumbling and waste of time as to lose us the race. Furthermore, even though we hoped we'd turned the lightship ahead of the *Belle,* we were fully aware that, because of her greater length, weight, and schooner rig, she could and would, outreach us on this leg of the course.

"A tight clinch, and no way out," I thought. And when a particularly heavy, steep sea hove the *Garland* over until her deck was awash to the skylight coaming, and I saw the Skipper's face harden as he strained on the tiller, all my "bubble-and-squeak" evaporated. It was serious business now, with no more cheering.

111

As it was with me, so, I suspect, it was with all hands during the hour and a half that followed our turn of the lightship. The cold iron of our situation had been driven home. No instant's loss of time by bungling or confusion could be tolerated. And it was in such mood that within fifteen minutes we had again "eased sheets to run her off for Noman's," as the Skipper explained, "before laying her onto a course for the whistler." Then, two at a time, commencing with Theoph and me, we'd gone below to sit braced on the cabin sole to "sup spoon vittles," as Cap'n Wasque described our hurried dispatch of the stew he served us in bowls which we wedged between our knees, while the *Garland* rolled and pitched unceasingly.

Back again on deck, I was called to take the helm while the Skipper and Captain Van Courtland had their "go at the prog" — a not altogether festive meal judging by the Commodore's face when they both reappeared. But short as their absence had been I was glad to have the Skipper nearby again; for I'd found the *Garland* a handful in the heavy going. Lord! How she'd rolled down and tossed the spray about as we yawed and bumped along. And how forlorn and feeble the bleating of our horn as we'd bored into the blinding smother!

Silent beside me on the steering bench, the Skipper concentrated his attention on the uneasy compass card and the hands of a big watch jammed in a waterproof case lashed to the base of the binnacle. When forty-five minutes had passed he ordered Willie to the foot of the mainmast to keep a sharp lookout to leeward, while Nils was sent aloft to the spreaders to keep an eye peeled out ahead and to windward.

Ten minutes went by without change or report from the lookouts, at which the Skipper shuffled his feet impatiently. Two minutes more ticked away — and then Nils hailed, and pointed to the sky ahead where the fog, becoming luminous, began to break up into tattered clouds, smoking away to the east, while the wind, shifting from my right cheek to the back of my neck, was noticeably drier than it had been.

"Let her come up to south, three-quarters west," said the Skipper to me, and followed this with a call to "haul aft," which brought Nils down from his perch on the run.

During the short time required to trim the sheets and bring the *Garland* onto her course, that puff of dry wind had eaten a hole in the gloom around us to the extent of perhaps a quarter of a mile, while overhead a feeble, spongy sun occasionally broke through the dull gray ceiling. Swiftly and mysteriously the horizon continued to expand, until a half mile to the southeast of us we could make out boulders on a beach smothered in spray and the overhanging bluffs at the west end of Noman's Land. "And that's a favor straight from heaven," said the Skipper gratefully. "And now if we ease her when she pitches and luff her when she rolls, we ought to hit that buoy on the nose in half an hour."

But this stretch proved hubbly going for the *Garland,* with the ebb tide cocking up the ocean seas into a big, nasty chop which had to be dealt with respectfully. Again and again it was a case of slowing her down to ease her over one that looked as if it would break on board. And to make more trouble for us and reduce our speed, the wind was unsteady — backing and hauling through several points — while patches of fog blowing by shifted the outlook confusingly.

The feeling had just come over me that unless we heard or sighted the buoy soon our goose was cooked, when I saw Nils poke his head above the rail and cup his ear with his hand, while from to windward came a faraway bleat of a vessel's foghorn. Within a couple of minutes there it was again, but louder and from farther ahead. And then once more the wind hauled in a dry squall, clearing a long corridor in the murk, down which, as we looked, the whistler bobbed into sight on the crest of a mile-away sea, while to the northwest the *Belle* burst into the clear, reaching for the mark.

At first glance 'twas a tossup which of us held the lead; but after a minute the Skipper settled the question by exclaiming:

"Damnation! We're euchred by playing it safe — she's got us by half a mile."

And so it proved to be; for, while we still bored our way close-hauled through those head seas, we were constrained to watch our big rival sail swiftly across the gap between us and the mark, swing up into the wind, trim her sheets smartly, come about, and stand away to the northwest on the port tack; while five minutes later, to the accompaniment of the buoy's dismal groaning, we tacked in her wake at fifteen minutes past noon.

Eight hours later the *Garland,* heading north, was close to a beach overhung by steep bluffs at the southwesterly end of Block Island. Under the urge of a fair tide and a gentle westerly breeze just strong enough to keep her sails asleep, she was reaching silently but swiftly through a narrow belt of rippling water that hugged the shore. To the west and south, beyond the influence of this little breeze, long ocean swells heaved languidly, reflecting on their glassy shoulders the crimson and gold of the twilight glow. It was a situation to gratify both spirit and flesh — and gaining it had not been easy, or, at times, without risk.

For there had been the hour when we had trailed the *Belle* in a seemingly hopeless stern chase during which, in spite of the fog's clearing, the sky to windward had darkened ominously as great thunderheads rolled up from the north, stirring the wind into vicious squalls. Higher and higher had towered the clouds in two columns which seemed destined to meet at the zenith. Sharper and sharper had shrilled the wind in the rigging, and more and more confusedly had run the seas until the *Garland* staggered drunkenly, while her crew, battered by spray, clung to her deck like drowning rats.

At last a sharp crack of lightning followed by the boom of thunder, and the order: "Hand the topsail, staysail, and jigger!" had galvanized all hands into violent action. It was in the midst of this flurry of slatting canvas and flying ropes that Nils confirmed his statement — "I ban good man when she blows" — by swinging himself aloft on the instant to clear the clew of the topsail, jammed in the bridle of the peak halyards. While we still fought to smother the flogging sails, the call had come to "tack ship" — and as the *Garland*'s head swung into the wind we had a moment's glimpse of the *Belle* out ahead, with her mainmast bare of sail.

It was at this moment of turmoil that our observer had crawled to the steering bench to shout: "Keep her off — keep her off! You can't stand out in such weather!" which so startled the Skipper that he snapped: "Can't stand out? Why the hell not — what d'ye think we came out here for?" — questions which went unanswered; for at that moment the Commodore was cut down by a violent bout of seasickness, after which, at a sign from the Skipper, Wasque helped him below.

Then, as the clouds met overhead, the Skipper had shivered the *Garland* through the fierce squall of wind and blinding rain which swept over her; and when this first overpowering blast had screamed off to leeward, he filled her away until she was heading a trifle south of west, sailing under her reduced rig with something like comfort in the strong breeze which had followed the squall from the same quarter.

For about two hours we had continued on this offshore board until, under a clearing sky, and finally sunshine, we tacked, as the wind moderated and backed to the southwest. Then, after shaking the reef out of the mainsail, we reset the staysail, gaff topsail, and jigger and shifted jibs — number 1 in place of number 2 — to start the *Garland* snoring away to westward with no trace of her competitor in sight.

Then had come a three-hour stretch of glorious sailing in a strong, whole-sail breeze, and after a while a long, easy sea, giving the *Garland* her first chance that day to tick off the miles without drenching us. And when the blue, misty outline of Block Island nicked the horizon ahead, we celebrated this landfall by shedding our soggy waterproofs to give the sun a go at drying us out.

But, as we'd closed with the land abreast of the harbor, the wind, coming offshore, had drawn ahead in a series of puffs, posing the problem of whether to turn the Island north about or south about — a riddle to "give a feller gray hairs, figurin' tides and weather," as Theoph had predicted. It was anybody's guess, but the Skipper's sole responsibility. And we waited in silence for his decision.

The first intimation that he'd made up his mind was his order to set the number 1 jib topsail, which was accomplished smartly and without a hitch. A few minutes passed, while the gaps between the offshore puffs lengthened — when it was: "Down with the gaff topsail and up with the jack yarder!" And when this had been completed and the *Garland* tacked — close to the beach, with her head to the south — we had the Skipper's answer to the puzzle.

This tack had been his first throw in a gamble to save a fair tide on the other side of the Island; and at times, during the trying two hours of play that followed, our chance to win seemed utterly hopeless. For, as the sun declined, so did the wind, until look where we might, except for a narrow ribbon of dark blue water close along the shore, the sea lay unruffled — while a foul tide gripped us relentlessly. Offshore and inshore, tack by tack, we crept along, clinging desperately on the edge of that little stir of air fanning off from the beach, until at last we worked up abreast of the high bluff from the top of which the tall Southeast lighthouse — dull red in the sunset — stared down at us. Then, with our goal actually in sight, the little breeze faded, leaving us lolloping without steerage way in a jobble of oily swells and backwash.

Minute after minute ticked away with no sign of change, when suddenly the Skipper, quoting our old friend the Portugee Pirate, had exclaimed:

"Every-theeng — God damn!"

116

Whereat, as if a barn door had blown open, a draft of warm air smelling of hay wafted down from the heights to fill the *Garland*'s sails and give her a new lease of life. Falteringly at first, but later with some heart, this new breeze continued coming on until long fingers of it darkened the water ahead. Steadily, yet still at a snail's pace, we edged away from the lighthouse — tack after tack — toward the headland on the turning of which all our acts and thoughts focused. And after what seemed an age, had come an order to shift jib topsails — assurance that we were about to weather the point and hear the welcome call: "Stand by to slack sheets and break out that ballooner!"

And so it had come about, just after the sun had set, that the *Garland* was reaching silently but swiftly through this narrow belt of rippling water, while the flood tide, with two hours still to run, was giving her a grand push on the home-bound leg.

It was at this auspicious moment, when we'd handed the jib and staysail and trimmed all sheets to a T, that Cap'n Wasque appeared in the companionway to announce "First call!" with his spoon and pan. Again it was a case of two at a time, beginning with Theoph and me. But what a difference between this and our last meal! For now, instead of bolting bowls of stew in pitching, rolling confusion, we sat comfortably at table while the Captain served hot loin of pork, roasted potatoes, boiled onions, and, to top off with, plum pudding and creamy hard sauce flavored with brandy — from my enjoyment of all which even the suggestive sight of a bucket below the berth where the Commodore lay, back toward us, detracted mighty little, if at all.

And then came our heyday in this race, when, as Theoph and I were on our way up to the deck, the *Garland,* stealing by a headland beyond which the coast trended to the northeast, opened a clear view far ahead, disclosing the *Belle* — a mile or more away, close-hauled on the inshore tack!

117

"What price *Garland* now?" roared Theoph.

"Rouse out the Commodore and bring him on deck, alive or dead!" called the Skipper; so that presently our observer (courageously, it seemed to me, for he looked far from hearty) had crawled aft to his post to stare with the rest of us at those distant, barely moving sails — rose-ash in the fading twilight.

Clear of the obstructing headland, the set of the tide, running truer and stronger, boosted the *Garland*'s pace so that within ten minutes she had drawn abreast of her competitor, who, hardly holding her own against the adverse current, faced an hour's delay waiting for slack water, unless in the meantime the wind freed for her or came stronger.

And as we slipped across and beyond her wake, the Skipper, as I relieved him at the helm, remarked: "Well! So far, so good, as the man said when he was half-way through cutting his throat; and, Commodore, how about a little dinner now?" Getting a shake of the head for answer, he ordered Nils and Willie to follow him below.

Twenty minutes later, with all hands on deck again, we jibed 'round the bell buoy off Sandy Point, set the spinnaker, and squared away on an east-three-quarters-north course for the run — as we hoped it might prove — of thirty knots to the Hen and Chickens lightship.

Very slowly, for the breeze continued light from the west, we drew away from the Island, until the bearing of the fixed light on Point Judith had shifted from northeast to north. Then, contrary to all expectation, the wind, instead of hauling, backed to west-southwest and came in stronger, causing us to trim sheets and guys again. After ten minutes' silent study of the weather, the Skipper said to me:

"Willie, Nils, and I are going below now for a caulk. Call us in two hours, or sooner if there's any change." So presently Theoph and the Commodore and I had the deck to ourselves. A little later Cap'n Wasque appeared with bowls of hot potato soup and our pea jackets — gifts greatly appreciated, even by Captain Van Courtland, in the chill of the now-heavy fall of dew.

Then for an hour the *Garland,* except for a gentle, rhythmic dip and rise, sailed silent and steady on an even keel; while a three-quarters moon pied the ruffling surface of the long seas. And finally, when I'd begun to feel bemused by the swings of the compass card under the dim light of the binnacle and the play of green glow reflected from our starboard running light on the leach of the spinnaker, I was startled to find the Commodore beside me on the steering bench.

"Feeling better, I hope, sir?" said I; to which he replied: "Who wouldn't, after such a grand race — and with this lovely moonlight now. But that sea off Noman's was a nasty one; too much for me, I'm ashamed to admit." And from then until it was time to call the other watch he laid himself out to entertain us — quite drawing the sting of his previous offish manner — with the log of a cruise he'd made in the Gulf of California.

When I'd given the Skipper the bearings of the lights then in sight, I went below and turned into my berth "all standing," to fall asleep instantly and be wakened only a minute later, as it seemed, by a commotion overhead and a call for "all hands!"

Responding on the run, I was met at the head of the ladder by a chilly darkness tainted with the smell of clammy mudflats, a dead calm, a jobble of sea, and the sound of limp canvas slamming and slatting. And as Theoph followed me out on deck, we heard the Skipper say:

"There's a breeze from the eastward on the way — so get those light sails off of her in a hurry!" — a command that sent me forward on the jump to help Nils and Willie hand the spinnaker and ballooner, while Theoph hauled aft the main and jigger sheets and tended the spinnaker-boom guy. In the midst of this hurrah's nest of confusion came a puff from the northeast, then another, and another, with shorter and shorter intervals between, until within fifteen minutes the *Garland* was laying down to a lively breeze close-hauled on the port tack, with the staysail set but the jib still to be hoisted — a beastly job before we were through with it, in the darkness and flying spray.

For half an hour, soaking wet and shivering in the cool wind, we lay on deck close under the weather rail, as the pale light of dawn crept up from the east to dim the stars and gray the sea, while the twin lights on Hen and Chickens lightship to windward contracted to bright pinpoints. Minute by minute the horizon broadened until, there ahead of us and fine on our lee bow, Cuttyhunk and Penikese islands loomed dark against the rosy sky, while to the north and east stretched the mainland.

As soon as we could weather the lightship, the *Garland* was tacked to stand away to the north, with the first of the flood tide under her port bow and the prospect of smoother water ahead in the lee of the weather shore — a seemingly good move under the conditions. And I had just conjured up the pleasing picture of the *Belle,* bucking a head tide and wind as I had last seen her — when, looking astern slightly to windward of our wake, I saw a schooner under a press of sail emerge from the gloom of Cuttyhunk. In a flash I recognized her and bawled the news that our rival was close on our heels; at which the Skipper, after a look over his shoulder, exclaimed:

"Confound that shift of wind to the south'ard last evening — it was just her meat and she's been overhauling us all night. This offshore breeze is as full of tricks as a bag of monkeys — better get that number 1 jib topsail on deck again, in case we have to use it in a hurry."

And so, after a hundred miles and more of hard sailing, and only ten miles left to go, the winning or losing of the race was still a tossup with time and the weather the imponderables. Again, as it had been at the start, minutes and seconds saved or lost were to be the prime factors — as we aboard the *Garland* soon realized. For, as we drew in toward the land, the wind first headed us, then eased so that we tacked offshore and set the topsail, only to have the breeze haul ahead and come strong again, forcing the Skipper to shiver her through the puffs; while farther out in the Bay, where conditions, it seemed, were less fickle, the *Belle* gained steadily until she was within a quarter of a mile and a little to windward of us.

At this moment — an exasperating one for us — with the breeze showing every sign of fading out, the *Belle* was tacked offshore, while we split with her to head inshore and weather Mishaum Point "by the flick of a minnie's tail," according to Theoph. Then a minute later came the familiar call, "Ready about — heard-a-lee!" and as the *Garland*'s head rounded slowly into the wind's eye the upper limb of the sun cleared the high land of Naushon Island, away to the eastward, while all around us spread glassy patches of calm, checkered with ruffling, dark-blue catspaws.

"And now," said the Skipper, motioning me to the helm, "it's dog eat dog; so I'll nip aloft and try a game of hopscotch with these zephyrs — and mind your Ps and Qs when it comes to tacking and handling sheets."

As to time and sequence of events during this, my last trick at the helm, I can give no accounting; for my recollection is of growing consciousness of an ache at the back of my neck as I stared upward in a tense pose, one eye on the luff of the mainsail and the other on the Skipper, perched — back to me — on the weather horn of the spreaders, from where there issued an interminable succession of calls to "keep her off — luff a little — steady as she goes — let her come — ease your sheets — flatten her down" — as he conned the *Garland* through the maze of calms and wandering puffs.

Incidentally, I recall that, as the sun climbed higher, the reflection from the glassy patches dazzled my eyes and caused them to water; that, by a miracle of prescience born of long experience, the Skipper, anticipating where the next breath of air was about to strike, slid the *Garland* from square to square of that constantly shifting chessboard without her losing steerage way at any time; that Theoph, Willie, Nils, and Cap'n Wasque,

121

and even the Commodore, caught up in the anxious excitement of this last act of ours, played their parts on the deck — precisely, silently, and with minimum of movement; that several times as we tacked I caught a fleeting glimpse of the *Belle,* without attempting to determine her position in relation to our own or whether she was becalmed or sailing; while at the same time the Dumpling Rock lighthouse slowly but surely bulked against a stretch of gently glinting blue water — a belt of breeze where, if we could but reach it, we might find release from the strain of dodging and doubling through these doldrums.

And finally and most vividly I remember, as we ghosted across a broad stretch of calm on the port tack with only the heads of the topsails alive and pulling, the exultant note in the Skipper's voice as he hailed the deck: "And once more, let her come!" followed by his slithering descent from aloft and taking over the tiller, just as the *Garland* filled away on the starboard tack.

After release from what seemed a lifetime of aching concentration, I took a long breath and then a look 'round, to find, to my astonishment, that we were to windward of the lighthouse and slipping by the Dumplings under the urge of a far-reaching finger of that so longed-for belt of breeze. And what was more, we were fetching — Yes, by God! — actually fetching White Rock, with the old *Theresa,* her brass cannon glinting in the sunshine, waiting patiently on station to proclaim the winner; while hardly more than two cable lengths to the southeast of us the *Belle* lay dead, her sails limp and drooping in a flat calm.

And as, by the favor of Aeolus, we continued to hold onto the hem of that so-modest breeze, which withdrew step by step with our oncoming, like turning back the pages of a book, I can still recall the sense of loss — almost of regret — that overcame me as I watched the gap of glassy calm widen inexorably between us and our lovely, courageous competitor — until suddenly this inexplicable mood was transmuted into exultation by the shattering thud of the gun announcing VICTORY!

NINE

Clambake

A S IF mortally stricken by the crash of the gun proclaiming *Garland* the winner of the match, the trickle of breeze which had wafted us across the finish line expired. Thereafter for the best part of an hour we lay "as idle as a painted ship" — encircled by a stillness that grew moment by moment as the warm sunshine filmed and muted our surroundings with shimmering heat-haze; until even in our exaltation we instinctively lowered our voices while discussing the race and the coffee and buttered biscuits that Captain Wasque served us as we sprawled on deck. And finally, when food and hot sun had combined to overcome us with drowsiness so that heads began to nod as the *Garland* was gently rocked by the almost imperceptible breathing of the calm water, the little windsock of blue bunting which drooped inert from the tip of the pole of the jackyard topsail suddenly lifted and commenced to flutter lightly. This stir of life was followed shortly by a draft of cool, damp air smelling of ocean, while off to the southwest the glassy surface of the Bay was streaked by a dark blue line —

the crisped and glinting van of a sea breeze — which came swiftly toward us.

A minute or so later, after a tremor or two had run rustling over her sails, the *Garland* had been overtaken by a forereaching puff of the oncoming true wind and was underway heading, not for Padanaram, but instead for the anchorage abreast of Beetle's Boat Yard on the east shore of Clark's Point. Still astern but overhauling us rapidly as she brought the breeze up with her came the *Belle,* to presently complete her course by crossing the finish line and then square away in our wake; while the *Theresa,* released from duty, followed a quarter of a mile behind.

A scant two hours later the *Belle, Theresa,* and *Garland* were lying quietly at moorings in the cove off the boat yard with sails furled and all shipshape — but deserted by their crews. For all hands, at the pressing invitation of the Skipper, had dropped the role of sailors to assume that of pilgrims to a shrine — a rough circle of clean, washed beach stones set in a clearing overlooking a sandy beach. The rite to be performed here, known as the "Cottage Clambake," was an annual celebration in which the Skipper presided as high priest; and, again in emulation of Steve Brodie, he had some weeks before fixed the day and hour of this year's "bake" on the off chance that, if Allah so willed, it might climax the finish of the match between the *Garland* and the *Belle* — and, as Luck has a way of smiling on the bold, he had won this race against time as well as the other.

As for me, alas! The Fates had decreed that I should part from my shipmates on landing to make a solitary, hot, and dusty journey to the city in order to report at the office early the following morning. But, in spite of keen disappointment, I had the memory of former celebrations to give me the vicarious satisfaction of partaking in the ritual, commencing early in the week with the hauling of cordwood — half green, half dry — and stacking it close to the circle of stones or "bake-hole" and, on the day before that appointed for the attendance of the pilgrims, the great activity that took place throughout the neighborhood.

For at morning low tide — no matter how early it may occur — two gangs spread themselves along the shores of the Cove, one with buckets and clam forks, the other with farm wagons and pitchforks, for the clams must be sweet, clean, and fresh, and the rockweed to bank the bake with, unwilted. The experienced diggers have no difficulty in producing, during one tide, the prescribed half peck of clams — not too big and not too small — for every expected guest and helper. These the boys free from their stains of black mud and sand, finally sousing the full buckets in clear pools of sea water to rinse the grit out of the "critters" before transferring them to an open-seamed barrel in the cart.

There is also abundance of crisp rockweed, with golden-brown juicy bladders bursting with brine, floating at water level and caught in the pools among the boulder-strewn fore-shores. This is forked into piles at the heads of little coves or on sandy beaches where a wagon can most nearly approach, then loaded on the wagon and drawn handy to the bake-hole, where it is stacked and covered with sheets of heavy canvas to hold in the brine and protect the weed from sun and dew.

The clams meanwhile, in the open-seamed barrel, together with several open-headed tight barrels of fresh sea water, are hauled to the cart shed, whose stone walls and tree-shaded roof will keep them calm and free from nervousness. Twice during the next twelve hours the clams are well sluiced down with bucketfuls of the fresh salt water.

While these preparations are in progress, Clark's Point farms are searched for muskmelons, and a bushel or more of fine green and golden globes are thumbed and smelled and found juicily ripe. These are picked and brought with care to The Cottage, where they are ranged on a broad, sunny shelf and, while still warm, are cored from one end to the center, care

125

being taken that the rind as cut shall be preserved whole, to be used as a plug after the core-hole has been filled with the incomparable Madeira that has gone a sailing voyage to the Far East and back to New Bedford. They are then set back on the shelf, plug end up, and allowed to chill all night, and before the morning sun has dried the icy dew on them they are set away in the coolest end of the cart shed — nectar and ambrosia — to await their appointed moment at the feast.

A gray sunrise on the day of ceremony assures good weather. The sweet corn is gathered early with the cool crispness of the night beaded on its green sheaths; the sweet potatoes are scrubbed, the small white onions pulled and stripped. The fish (rock cod for preference), taken the day before and kept alive during the night in a fish car, are gutted and, with heads, fins, tails, and skins left on, are lowered into the cool, shadowy shaft of the well in a basket that has been carefully scalded and scrubbed and allowed to dry out in the sun.

Ten-thirty A.M. to the dot is the hour set for lighting the fire in the bake-hole; for heat — and plenty of it — is to reach the vitals of its sides and encircling beach stones, and a heavy bed of embers is to be laid down on its bottom before it will be ready for the sacrifice. Much care and time, backed by experience, will be expended on this pyre, for when the match is applied at the appointed hour it must instantly burst into rushing flame in every part — circumference as well as middle. First is laid down a good heavy bed of old dry-as-tinder hay, with a train leading up to and outside the circle of stones. Above this is constructed a framework of soft-pine fagots, dry but with the pitch still sticky, so placed and braced with air spaces between the crossed sticks that it will neither flatten down and smother the bed of hay below it nor be broken down by the weight of the oak and maple logs that are ranged in grids above it — first a grid of split dry wood, then one of green, and so on until there is only space enough left for two more layers of fuel to top the encircling and containing boulders. The first of these last two layers is then heavily ballasted with clean, wave-washed stones about the size and shape of coconuts, above which the last grid of logs is placed — an arrangement that assures space for ample oxygen to mix with the gas and smoke coming from the fire below and play upon the ballast stones, forcing into them a special intensity of heat.

To the youngest helper should always be accorded the privilege of setting the train alight. For in the years to come he will never lose the memory of that particular match, its almost explosive results, and the events that followed.

While the fire roars and crackles, eating up the hardwood fuel to convert the bake-hole into a volcanic crater and heat the stones to shimmering incandescence, white-pine planks that are kept on hand for these occasions are set up on wooden horses to form a rough table in the shape of a hollow square, with benches running along both its outer and inner sides. This table is so placed that it is to windward of the fire, and after the sun passes the meridian and slopes toward the west it will be dappled with shade from the trees on the edge of the clearing. The end toward the bake-hole is not completed, allowing service to be rendered easily and quickly to all quarters.

Leaving an experienced aide armed with a rake with a long iron handle to tend the fire, the Skipper and two of his crew enter the cart shed where the green corn and sweet potatoes have been keeping cool. There the ears are stripped down to the last two of their pale, straw-colored cerements, and the tassel silk is carefully picked off, leaving the old-ivory kernels enwrapped against smoke or contamination while in the bake. The fish, cold and firm-fleshed, are then fetched to the shed from the well shaft and treated to a seasoning of pepper and salt, well rubbed in both outside and in the gaping belly cavity; and a sprig of costmary (that herb of all others intended by Heaven to add a fillip to a baked fish) is inserted between the flaps of the gash; and finally all of them are carefully wrapped in the tenderest inner fronds of corn husk.

At noon the fire at the bake-hole has ceased to seethe with flames and has become a deep sea of glowing coals, reddening and whitening as the puffs of southwest wind blow over its surface, beneath which the ballast stones have sunk to the bottom and lie white-hot, many of them ready to crack open when their covering of embers is presently removed by the help of long-handled besoms and gray birch twigs.

Now has arrived the crucial moment in the ceremony, for every minute and movement counts in the preservation of the highest possible temperature in and around the bake-hole. The instant the last hot coal or smouldering ember that might poison the bake with acrid smoke has been brushed out and away, the pile of rockweed is stripped of its canvas covering, and dripping forkfuls of it are thrown into and around the hole and pushed and prodded to form a shallow nest above the white-hot bottom stones and up the shelving sides of the circle. Onto this cushion, which for a few moments only remains wet and steamless, the potatoes in their scrubbed jackets and the corn and fish in their corn-husk wrappings are spread, while the clams in their glistening white papery shells are poured in among them and leveled off — all done with the precision of a gun crew on a battleship in action, under the eye and tense instruction of the Skipper.

During this loading of the bake, two of the crew stand by with the canvas sheet that has covered the pile of rockweed, and as the last of the clams are settled they clap the canvas over the top of the nest, tucking the clams and their companion bedfellows snugly and cleanly away. More rockweed is then forked on until all signs of the bake-hole and what it holds in its heart are lost to sight.

Only fifty-six minutes are now left before it is time to uncover the bake. Every one of these minutes is precious, for there is much still to be done to set the stage for the shift, without a letdown, from anticipation to realization. The acolytes are divided into two crews, "youngs" and "olds" — the former to act as Ganymedes and Hebes for the duration of the day; the latter to assist the womenfolk of the household in the kitchen and later at the bake-hole. Each division has a captain who knows the ropes and whose word is law. Under such military ordering it is but a short time before the table in the clearing is furnished with the requisite number of knives and forks, coarse linen napkins of generous size and laundered soft, Sandwich-glass tumblers, maplewood bowls (capacity about a quart) — and, on the ground under the edge of the table, to the right of every indicated seat, an empty bucket. To windward of the bake-hole on a washtub bench are four well-scoured maple chopping trays, empty.

Within doors both summer and winter kitchens are in full blast, the latter redolent with the steam of the onions that have just been poured into kettles of walloping water on the range, while on an iron rack over the cookstove of the summer kitchen stacks of glazed heavy earthenware plates and shallow bowls are heating, and the sweet, unsalted, freshly churned butter is slowly liquefying in a saucepan on the end of the stove farthest from the firebox. A moment arrives when, at a given signal, an iron door in the chimney breast next the range is swung open and the dark umber loaves of brown bread (in the dough of which only that soft, gray Rhode Island cornmeal ground between slow-turning stones in an old water- or wind-driven gristmill, and dark, heavy West India molasses are tolerated) are drawn out on long-handled wooden paddles from the cavern of the blandly hot brick oven where for hours they have been slowly baking. Hot to their very cores, they are lined up on clean hardwood cutting boards and swathed in fresh linen napkins to preserve their moist sponginess and protect them from the assaults of flies and wasps.

In ample time to arrive without any sensations of hustle or bustle, the pilgrims begin to make their appearance in the wide-track, two-seated "wagons" as the carriages with standing tops and furling side curtains of this countryside are called.

After discharging their passengers, who move off to the lee side of the bake-hole, the drivers maneuver the wagons into the shade cast by the farm barn, loose the traces, and lead the horses to a long rack for hitching, then join their friends in the clearing. There is a good reason for choosing this position during the short wait before the uncovering takes place, for wafted downwind come odors from that heap of rockweed that would whet the most jaded appetite, but in hungering pilgrims arouse ecstasies of anticipation.

When only ten more minutes are left before the appointed time, several stone jugs are hoisted from the well shaft where they have been suspended all morning and, sweating with the sudden change from cool to warm, take central positions on the table. This is the signal for the pilgrims to be seated — which is done without haste or jostling, for there is room and to spare for all at this board. The jugs are then uncorked and circulated from hand to hand clockwise (disaster would follow if they moved against the sun), with a pause above every tumbler, into which is poured a "jorum" of pale, amber-colored liquid, cold but not overchilled, the ingredients of which are one third white Santa Cruz rum, a third strained juice of Dominica limes, and the balance slightly sweetened smoky China tea, with a suspicion of bruised mint leaves. This brew, of which only a sip should be taken before the clams make their appearance, is called locally "Lime Calabash," the wherefore being a yarn by itself of good length and much action.

This first libation has no sooner been poured than there issues from the house a procession — the Skipper and his entire crew — which bears down on the clearing all loaded with impedimenta: baskets of hot plates and bowls, hot pitchers of melted butter with a dash of cayenne pepper, hot steaming bowls of onions in a thin sauce of milk with a speckling of black pepper, cutting boards with the veiled loaves of brown bread, and a stack of cold plates and dessert spoons for serving at their proper moment those melons still hidden modestly in the shed.

The Skipper now takes his place close to the mound of rockweed with watch in hand, supported by four of the "olds."

"Fifty-five," he calls, and at this signal two of the trusty four start pitching forkfuls of the rockweed to one side; and as the pile dwindles and the canvas blanket is neared, wisps and jets of delicious-smelling steam pervade the clearing, a compound of odors impossible to describe but, once enjoyed, never to be forgotten. As the last forkfuls are lifted from the steam-stained canvas, the besoms are passed over the surface to rid it of remnants of the weed, which the heat has transformed to shreds and twigs, lustreless and brittle. Then the blanket is gingerly seized at the two corners to leeward, lifted up, and turned back, exposing enough of the bake to allow the two acolytes with the toughest labor-callused hands to kneel and flip the infernally hot clams into the chopping trays, which four of the "youngs" are tendering like begging bowls. The four trays, brimming full, are then rushed to the table and discharged into the wooden bowls in front of the pilgrims and the now-seated Skipper.

A neophyte at this point might be puzzled as to what the correct procedure might be, but not so with this band of seasoned veterans, for they fall to with claw and tooth, shucking off the white shells, lifting the tender sweet morsel therefrom, stripping the skin from the shrunken black snout, and then, with a dextrous dip into the bowl of melted butter, popping the clam whole into hungering mouths. Most of the shells, after the clams have been lifted out, will contain a spoonful of salty liquor or broth; this also should be tilted into the mouth after each swallow. The empty shells are dropped into the buckets on the ground.

The first bowl of clams disappears with surprising speed. Another relay appears, reinforced with fish, corn, and potatoes from the bake, and slices of brown bread and helpings of onions from the center of the table. But from this point on how can I attempt to set down in words, which after all are poor things, the disposal of all these gifts of God, which have been for the most part cooked in the good earth, seasoned by the salts thereof, uncontaminated by the impurities of civilization, fresh as the dawn, and in such abundance that no one has to bolt his first helping to ensure a second, third, or even a fourth — except to say that, when every soul here gathered has filled himself or herself to comfortable capacity and those who smoke have ignited the butt ends of Manila cheroots that have come tied in bunches with buttercup-yellow ribbands in leaden chests from the Far Eastern Isles, the day sinks softly and peacefully down toward its end in a pale blue smoky haze of contentment: a contentment that can come only from the know-how of making the most of Nature's gifts and the satisfaction arising from such knowledge, which has been acquired, not from endowed institutions of learning, but from attendance at that greatest of all universities, the outdoor world.

TEN

Thumblings

I WAS EIGHTEEN, and as youngest member of the staff of a State Street, Boston, office had been left alone to close up on a Saturday afternoon of late winter. Outside, a drizzle — half snow, half rain — mingled with the sooty slush underfoot. I was growing both bored and lonely when the postman shoved a letter through a slot in the door. I read my name in the superscription and noted the official atmosphere that stamped the missive. So strongly did it smack of courts and lawyers that I slit the envelope reluctantly, to draw out a slip of paper on which was much printing in a minute type under the bolder caption:

COMMONWEALTH OF MASSACHUSETTS

Bristol SS

Probate Court

Which confirmed my foreboding that through some care-lessness "thousands had disappeared," for which I was now to be held accountable.

Thoroughly shaken, I extracted a second sheet that was neatly folded in the envelope. Spread open, this too proved to be a printed notice — but with a bank check to my order, in the amount of five hundred dollars, tucked away in it. My scalp prickled as, holding my fortune tightly, I began to read the legal phrasing of the printed form.

Translated into honest English it meant that a "Cornelius Howland et al.," owners of the ship *Fox,* had suffered the loss of this vessel and her cargo in 1798 by the unlawful act of a French man-of-war, and that now, after the lapse of a hundred years, restitution in part for this seizure had been given to me. There was mystery about this business. I felt I could not sleep without an explanation. The answer, I knew, could be had in New Bedford — and a half-hour later I was on board the evening train that would land me there before bedtime.

I have never enjoyed two hours more, for during the entire journey I was spending my money over and over again in imagination, only to find the windfall still intact on my arrival at the New Bedford depot. I felt so opulent that I hired one of the hacks that met every train to carry me over the four miles of cobbled streets and sandy roads to "The Cottage."

"Why, hang it all, my boy, " said the Skipper as I explained as well as I could the story of my incredible fortune, "we must build a new *Fox!* Your great-great-grandfather, the owner of the little ship in that notice of yours, would want you to do it — for he loved the sea and all that goes with it. I've heard him tell the whole story — how 'those frog-eating French rascals,' as he called them, in a big black frigate bore down on the little *Fox,* his first command, when she was on a West India voyage. They sent her into Fort-de-France with a prize crew aboard and sold her and the cargo out from under him without a by-your-leave. It riled him clear to the bottom and he would never quit pressing the claim for damages, although it cost him more than it was worth in the end — and now here at last, through you, he's squared accounts. I know he's rubbing his hands and chuckling with pleasure. Now let's see to it that the new *Fox* is a credit to the old gentleman."

Then, without waiting for any comments, the Skipper pulled out his drafting board, scale rule, tracing paper, French curves, and thumb tacks, and within an hour we were deep in the problems of the new ship's design. Before I started on my return journey to Boston next day we had arranged with Charles Beetle, the proprietor of Beetle's Boat Yard, to build our new *Fox* with all possible dispatch.

For the next six months I spent every Saturday night that I could at The Cottage, and Sundays at the boat yard. Here, when they could spare the time, the Skipper and Charles Beetle joined me and put in many hours of their skilled labor on the new boat. We three had some hand in every part and detail as she grew. We were intimate with the scarfs, mortises, tenons, and fastenings that were worked into the well-seasoned, pasture-grown white oak of the keel, stem, sternpost, and deadwood. We set up molds, we ran battens, we bent steamed timbers into place. We worked out garboard strakes and planking from a parcel of clear Gulf cypress. We selected the stock of native white cedar from which the five-eighths-inch ceiling was sawed. We spent much time and thought on the layout belowdecks — and yet, in spite of the fact that she was the product of their experience and skill, of their time, and, as I now suspect, of a considerable amount of their money, those two good friends of mine succeeded in maintaining in me the pride of creation and ownership.

Planned for singlehanded cruising in all seasons and weather, she was twenty-three feet overall, with short ends and seven-foot beam. All her ballast was outside — on her keel. She was flush-decked except for a small self-bailing steering well. Access to belowdecks was through a hatch with a slide — light and ventilation by means of a skylight. She was ketch rigged.

At last, late in September, a Saturday was chosen for the launching and for a holiday from the office for me. I was up and out of The Cottage early that day to take an observation. The yellow light of the dawn and the freshness of the air gilded and crisped the entire landscape — it was the first morning of a reborn world with the weariness and dust of the old one swept away. And as I came on a run to the little rise that sloped sharply down to the beach on the margin of which the boat yard sprawled, there, freed from the constricting walls of the building shed, lay my *Fox* in her cradle. For the first time I saw her in true perspective. Bow on, she seemed breasting her way up the gentle slope — risen but that moment from the water — and coming to greet me. To my astonishment, in the week I'd been away her masts had been stepped, her bowsprit run out, her standing rigging set up, her running rigging rove, and her tanned working sails bent.

Surprise mounted as I finally climbed on board and inspected her down below, where the same order as on deck was evident, even to the kindlings and coal in the fuel locker. All the gear requisite was on board and stowed, including a replica in proper scale of the family "house flag" that for three generations had been flown throughout the seven seas. I lost all count of time as I investigated, and I must admit I grew a shade jealous at the thought that the Skipper had had all the fun of assembling that equipment. With a sense almost of wrongdoing, I looked up to the hatch to see the Skipper's face framed in the opening smiling down at me.

"It's nine o'clock," said he, "and if you can spare the time, we might sit here in the cockpit for a minute and discuss the balance of the day." I ran up the ladder, and as I dropped into the well he handed me a basket. "Here's a bite of breakfast Debby insisted I must bring you — and Lord how she grumbled over the trouble menfolks and boats make around a house."

This was heaping coals of fire with a vengeance, and as I started in on the toast, tea, and crisp rashers that came out of the basket I tried to think how I could ever tell him how pleased, grateful, contrite — and all — I felt.

"Don't try to say it," he said as he watched me. "Charlie Beetle and I have had even more fun out of building her than you have."

"And now," he continued, "if you'll hustle back to The Cottage with the basket, you'll find there's a chance to square yourself with Debby and give Willie a hand with a job of work I've left him to do. I'll stay here to make sure the old railway's in shape so that when we let her go at high tide she'll slide."

When I reached The Cottage I found Deborah the cook in command. She immediately drove me out of the house to help Willie and Levi take the seats out of the spring wagon and begin to load it in the cool of the carriage house. The first item was a heavily built case marked "Pol Roger 1894"; then came a hamper with linen and another with glass and crockery; a plate-basket with table silver; two big chafing dishes with their hot-water baths and a jug of spirits for their lamps. By the time we had Billy Bowlegs, the old horse, harnessed and flicking his ears with curiosity at the stir of things, Debby was shouting from the kitchen door for us to make haste and bring the wagon there.

Passing through the kitchen to the scullery, to which place she ordered us, I saw that Deborah was very busy frying "thumblings" — small croquettes about the size of a big man's thumb — in two kettles of deep fat, and that a glazed bowl lined with a napkin stood warming in the mouth of the open oven, half full of the finished product. At that moment her back was toward the range, so I popped one of these thumblings. It was fiery hot, but I managed to hold onto it until I could trust it in my mouth, when I found, as I'd hoped, it was composed of a batter of mashed potato, shredded salt codfish, a mere trace of garlic, and cream — all whipped into a consistency that could be rolled into shape between the palms of the hands and then treated to a coating of finely crushed cracker crumbs and beaten yolk of egg and lastly dusted with flour.

By the time there were four bowls full of these thumblings all wrapped in linen, the two boys and I had transferred from the scullery to the wagon a big pine-staved tub of chipped ice, four wooden pails, and two smaller tubs in the middle each of which was a big wooden bowl of lettuce hearts and skinned tomatoes — half red and half yellow — and two tight-capped jars of mayonnaise all packed round with ice and carefully covered with clean cloths. Deborah insisted on superintending the loading of her precious thumblings, before dispatching us to Beetle's with the parting broadside: "Lord love yer if you upset things — for, like Queen Charlotte, I never will."

It was obvious now that doings were to take place at the shop and that the Skipper, as I might have known, was not going to let the *Fox* slip unnoticed down the ways. Her launching was to be colorful; and as a proof of it, when we came in sight of the yard both she and the buildings were gay with bunting — the many flags snapping in the now brisk breeze.

By noon, under the vigorous leadership of Charlie Beetle and the Skipper, the construction shed had been swept and tidied and a long trestle table with benches on each side and a chair at the head and the foot had been set up. The polished copper chafing dishes, one at each end of the table, gleamed richly pink in the reflected light from the white tablecloth, while the expanse between was relieved by the two salad bowls with their cool, brittle contents of yellow, green, and scarlet. In the measured center of the table rested a three-foot scale model of the Beetle Whaleboat, the acknowledged acme for craft of her kind. The big tub of chopped ice stood in a corner in the shade, the gilt-capped necks of the black champagne bottles sticking out invitingly.

Soon after twelve our first guest, Mrs. Beetle, arrived in the shop, leading a troop of boys and girls, all bearing gifts — loaves of waterbread so light of heart that they were straitjacketed in thick, brittle glazed crusts; pats of primrose-colored butter; a pair of New York State cheeses mellowed by some secret process, and several jars of her celebrated chowchow.

Within fifteen minutes a host of friends — twenty-two in all — were on hand, none without some offering. Job Almy, the sailmaker, had made a beautifully knotted bottle net to protect us against flying splinters when the actual christening of the *Fox* took place. John Sherman, who had dubbed out with his adze and broadaxe the keel, stem, and sternpost, brought a blue bowl of damson plums. Aunt Rachel, our beloved Quakeress, in a pearl-gray dress, poke bonnet, and white, lacy shawl, was followed by Joshua, her coachman, carrying a black and gold lacquered tray on which was a jar of candied ginger surrounded with lemon meringue tartlets shaped and sized to be handled whole — a single mouthful. And, that our other senses besides taste might be titillated, Obed Handy, the shipsmith, had fetched his accordion; while the shop itself, warmed by the midday sun, contributed delicious wafts of fragrance from the barrels of white cedar shavings swept from the floor.

Then the Skipper led Aunt Rachel to her chair at the head of the table and took his place at the foot; a champagne cork popped; everyone else found a seat, and thumblings hot from the chafing dishes began to flow with the sun. If there had been any unease among that various company, it was driven away by this time — not to return; and if kindliness and harmony among the sponsors at a launching have influence on the fortunes of a ship, the *Fox* was blessed that day.

But inexorably the sun sloped toward the west, the tide rose, and the moment came for us to leave the shop and perform the ceremony for which we'd gathered. When we were all on our feet, but before a move had been made toward the door, the Skipper signed to Golconda, and that gray-haired Kanaka whaleman and boss caulker immediately filled the cavernous building with the music of his sweet, true, falsetto voice. His choice of songs that day was "Rolling Home," the English chantey that commences:

> Fare ye well, Australia's daughters,
> For it's time for us to go.

And such is the effect of the spirit of the grape, when accompanied by good food and friendly faces, that all hands put their hearts into "Rolling Home" when Obed pumped his bellows to lead the chorus. Every eye glistened with sentiment as the final "Rolling Home, dear land to thee" faded and we filed out into the sunshine to form a semicircle round the bows of the *Fox*.

At this moment the Skipper whispered to me, "You climb aboard and go down with her." Then, turning to Aunt Rachel, he gave her a hand up onto a low trestle that raised her to the level of the boat's deck. Here she stood above the rest of the company, her gentle old face lighted with the excitement of what she was about to do. Taking the bottle in its net which Job handed to her, and with a tingle of color in her cheeks, she raised it, brought it down smartly with a crack on the bow chock, and as the foam sprayed out and ran creaming down the stem she called out:

"I christen thee *Fox* — little ship; and may thee always run as swiftly and as cannily as thy namesake, Reynard!"

With the report of the bursting bottle I felt a tremor run through the *Fox* as I stood expectant in the cockpit — and in another moment she and I were trundling down the beach, to be lifted presently from the cradle as if by strong arms and lie gently rocking on the clear water of the Acushnet estuary.

It took a minute or two for me to recover my breath from the crowding events of this faultless launching and to realize that a "singlehander" makes inordinate and constant demands on her crew. With what speed my unfamiliarity with the new gear would allow, I loosed the sails, hoisted them, and ran the house flag to the mainmast head — at which moment came the boom of a cannon. Startled, I looked toward the yard, to find it hidden in a cloud of white smoke which, drifting slowly to leeward, finally revealed my friends lined up along the beach, waving me farewell — with the Skipper a little apart, his outflung arm plainly signaling that the *Fox* and I were to make the trial trip alone.

And so, with sheets trimmed for a reach out to the Bay, the little ship gathered headway, while I was exalted by this further proof of the Skipper's deep and understanding generosity.

ELEVEN

Sim

ON A MID-JUNE morning two hours after sunrise the Skipper and I, on board my little singlehanded cruising boat *Fox*, were nearing the anchorage — a roadstead open to all but southerly winds — at the island of Noman's Land.

On the launching day, late in September of the previous year, I had made a bargain with the Skipper that he should be the first to cruise with me and that we should visit Noman's for a box of Jethro Gifford's salt codfish. And now here we were, thawing out in the warmth of a clear morning after a breezy night's sail that had chilled the very marrow in our bones. The Island in all its early summer greenery looked welcoming.

As we came close under the land we passed to leeward of a double-sprit rigged Island fishing boat with one man aboard her. In a big, hearty voice that balanced well with the rest of him he sang out to us:

"Father's ashore there, Skipper, and'll be glad to see you. I'll

underrun a trawl and be back again by noon — make your-
selves to home."

"That's Jethro," said the Skipper as he waved his arm in
acknowledgment of the hail, "and it's good news his father's
ashore; he's the world's champion man of iron, and if he'll talk
you'll hear a yarn worth a trip 'round Cape Horn."

Within a half hour we had anchored off the landing place, a
little beach of white sand, and I had launched the *Peapod,* my
six-foot punt, and brought her alongside ready to go ashore. It
was with some doubt as to her carrying us both that we cau-
tiously lowered ourselves into this cockleshell and, sitting back
to back, let her drift out and away from the *Fox.*

Finding we had an inch or more freeboard, I took up the
short oar and started to scull quietly, when the Skipper without
so much as turning his head said: "She'll do, I think, if neither
of us cough or sneeze," and so with "wanton heed and giddy
cunning" we brought her to the land.

Toting the *Peapod* between us, we set her down on the dry
sand well above high-water mark. Straightening up to look
around I saw a giant in faded blue shirt and overalls hurrying
toward us. "Sven of the Forkèd Beard grown old," thought I, as
he came near enough for me to see the silvery, double-pointed
beard and a pair of hot blue eyes tamed and a shade bewil-
dered by life's experience. But in spite of a helplessly palsied
right hand that he tried to control in his waistband, I could feel
strength and abiding courage in the grip of the great left hand
he gave me in greeting.

"Sim," said the Skipper, "we've come over on the chance we
can see those black ducks nesting and carry home a box of
Jethro's salt cod — and how have you all wintered over here?"

"I can show yer them ducks, Skipper, if ye feel like walkin' a
piece. An' as for the folks, we're all in good health an' thankee
kindly — includin' a new baby girl that arrove about a month
ago. Viola, we call her, 'count of her comin' the day the dog-
tooth violets blossomed. But Cortes, that infernal Kanaka, he's

up to his same old tricks. I seen him yesterday dodgin' 'round lookin' mournful at me as if he wanted to be friendly, but do what I could, I couldn't come nigh him. He hides on me, Skipper! An' by the Great Hook Block, I'm gettin' sort o' riled up with his antics," and Sim turned to look furtively behind him as if he'd felt a presence stealing up, while the Skipper looked at me and tapped his forehead. Turning back to us, Sim said:

"Would it pleasure you to go now to see them ducks an' then come back to the house for some dinner with us — for Dicey [short for Boadicea, Jethro's wife] she'd never forgive any of us if ye was to go off without seein' Viola."

"Good!" said the Skipper. "That suits us — so lead away!"

Sim was an inspiring guide to follow that morning, for as if turning the pages of a miraculous picture book he exposed the secrets of every dip, rise and twist of our path. There was a hummingbird's nest clamped in the crotch of a wind-shorn, stunted gray poplar; a bumblebee's hole in a sandy bank laced with crimson runners of wild strawberry; a vista that opened across a reed-rimmed pool the color of old brown sherry, to end in a wedge of blue ocean between two distant hillocks of green; and, as if to refresh us and add to the pleasure of sight, innumerably shy blossoms of wild flowers — some of them subtropical aliens — together with patches of bayberry which, warmed by the strengthening sunshine, added their fragrance to that of the salty breeze.

"Frankie Drake and his Lady," as Sim called the pair of black ducks we had come across the Island to see, were very much at home when we came to their pitch. While keeping a wary eye on the Skipper and me, they waddled fearlessly over and around Sim's feet, waggling their short, perky tails and greeting him with friendly, marshy voices as he dribbled cracked corn from one of his pockets. The grass around them — half last year's dead dun and half this year's tender green — seemed blown about with little whirlwinds, until I suddenly saw a fluff of pale yellow, streaked with brown, scuttle across a tiny

bare spot, and realized that the agitations came from the cease-
less activities of the brood of, Sim told us, eight ducklings.

At first glance this grassy slope near the crest of the highest
headland, from which the land broke sheer to the south beach,
seemed a most indefensible spot for a duck's nest. But with the
suddenness of magic the birds disappeared as the shadow of an
osprey circling out to sea skimmed across the hillside. And Sim
remarked:

"Trust black ducks to know their business. Gould an' Vander-
bilt wouldn't stand a chanst in a tangle with 'em. Them city
sharks'd starve if ducks was all they could get at to pluck." And
at the end of the half-hour that we watched this competent
family we had to agree with Sim.

Leaving the ducks, Sim brought us to the height of land,
from which we had a bird's-eye view of the entire Island.
Slowly boxing the compass with his eyes, the Skipper said as he
sat down:

"Sim, I somehow can never feel sure when I'm here whether
I'm a giant in a small country or a pygmy in a big one. Here's a
continent that we can see the whole of at a glance, which leaves
me uncertain. But there's one thing I *am* sure of, and that is, I'd
rather be here than on that floe you spent some time on —
back in '71, wasn't it? — on the Northwest Coast chasing
bowheads. What's your opinion of it?"

"Well," said Sim after a long pause, while his eyes roamed
over the folded country that lay between us and the white
landing beach with its ragged fringe of weather-worn cabins,
"there's been considerable wind blow by me since that time an'
my opinion's growed to a tolerable heft" — and then for an
hour he held us spellbound as he set before us the tale of his
odyssey of a month or more and the simple philosophy he had
evolved from this experience. It was obviously the very core of
his life. The years before and since were but the web of an
intensely practical dream, with the fitful appearances of Cortes,
his Kanaka boatsteerer, the only misplaced and tangled thread.

We shared with him that morning the tedious, anxious voyage of sixty days from San Francisco through Seventy-Two Pass into Bering Sea — much of it a beat in bitterly cold weather with northerly gales. We felt the growing irritation of all hands at the exceptionally adverse conditions; our "bile soured down" with Sim's "till there warn't nothin' in mind except to get fast to somethin' alive to kill."

And so it came about on a June morning, in spite of the heavy ice and infrequent leads of open water that were inclined to "pinch off," that Sim "beezled" Captain Jones into letting him lower his boat to hunt a whale that had been raised from aloft "off yander beyond considerable ice." And as they shoved off from the ship Captain Jones had said:

"Mister, if you've got to be a damned fool, I'd ruther you'd be one off this ship than aboard her. All I hope is God Almighty'll larn you some sense today — an' don't you lose nothin' more than your temper or I'll cut your comb for yer!"

Uncounted hours of Arctic daylight followed as Sim relentlessly drove his crew of five men in an attempt to gain the open water where it was hoped the quarry might be met. Miles of devious channels were explored, leading sometimes to windward and often to leeward, with the ship finally lost to sight and the direction in which she lay but a conjecture. There came a time when Sim himself was forced by cold and spent energy to allow he was "beat," and to put his mind to getting aboard the ship again. And then, as Sim put it, "the wind chopped 'round to the east'ard an' petered out," while the ice, which had tended to pack, loosened and cleared off, leaving the boat in a rapidly widening area of open sea. Under these changed conditions the boat was left to drift while Sim "figgered a traverse of where we'd come to."

Resting on their oars in silence, Sim and his crew were suddenly startled by an enormous sigh as a whale broke water almost alongside, exhaling her long-held breath in a double column of feathery steam that plumed seven feet or more into the chilly air. Gone in a twinkling was the weariness of the laborious hours; the oars were shipped, the paddles wielded, and still in profound silence the boat stole alongside that islet of black flesh, with Cortes balanced in the bows ready to strike.

"An' he got home good with the first iron," said Sim, "an' he shoved in his second clean up to the hitches, an' we was fast. Then she sounded till she'd run out 'most two tubs o' line — when up she come a-tearin' an' raced off into the eyes of a heavy squall o' wind an' snow that come drivin' from the north'ard. 'Haul!' says I, an' we all hove on that line to raise the dead. But gain much on her we couldn't an' the spray begun to fly."

At this stage of the hunt — a "Nantucket sleighride" — Cortes had come aft to take the long steering oar and Sim had gone forward into the bows to stand by until, finally alongside the whale, he could shove the long razor-edged lance into her vitals and direct the maneuvering of the boat during the death flurry. Blinded by the spray and oblivious to all else except gain on the line, he failed to see a "growler" (a small pan of ice) that lay just afloat in the body of an approaching wave. Jumping from crest to crest with a third of her length out of water, the boat met a sharp tongue of this ice with no more than a tremor, but with the appalling result, as Sim described it, that "her belly was slit from gills to vent."

Sickeningly aware of the deadly peril into which he had betrayed the lives and property for which he was responsible, Sim yanked a knife from its sheath, tacked on the "box" for such emergency, and in one stroke severed the straining whale line. This sudden parting of the rope threw the men off balance, an untimely wave crest caught the already staggering, half-waterlogged boat under her port bilge, and over she rolled.

Twenty minutes later Sim was tasting the bitter dregs of despair and contrition; for in spite of his coolheaded and untiring efforts to encourage — bullying here, cajoling there, and always ready with a hand or supporting shoulder — he had to see his struggling crew lose heart and strength in the icy water and one after another let go a slippery hold on some part of the overturned boat or her gear, until Cortes and he were left alone.

And here it became difficult to follow Sim's account, time and sequence shifting crazily while Cortes flitted about, a dreaded and pursuing specter at one moment, a warmly alive and loved companion at another, repelling every advance toward contact. One thing alone was clear — that Sim, to anchor his hold, shoved his right hand through the plug strap and succeeded in pulling himself and perhaps Cortes onto the boat's bottom astraddle of the keel so that, as he described it, "thar he sot an' thar I sot an' thar we both sot an' it growed almighty cold."

How long they "sot thar" and what transpired until Sim found himself alone, lying in slushy snow beside a "litter o' kindlings" — the utterly smashed boat — has to be guesswork. Undoubtedly Sim, and Cortes if he was there, lost consciousness within a few minutes, in which state Cortes would have been washed from his perch and drowned, while Sim, held firmly by the plug strap would have stayed with the boat until the wind and sea crashed her on a shelving spur of a providentially large and solid floe.

"An' I riz to my knees," said Sim, "an' I give a look 'round. But exceptin' for ice, there warn't nothin' solid or comfortin' in sight. Then way off yander, dodgin' round among the hummocks, I seen Cortes an' I hollered and hollered, but he didn't come no nigher, so I made shift to get onto my legs an' tried to run him down — but I was so stiff I wallered round like an old cow in a swale hole. Then I warmed up some an' could move pretty good, but the faster I went, the more Cortes doubled an' dodged on me, till I guess I lost my head an' begun to run an' beller, blind-crazy. When I was well wore out an' sweatin' scared, I says to myself: 'Sim! Quit bein' all kinds of a fool now an' forever, an' go back to what's left of the boat an' set a spell an' think'; an' so I done."

The result of this spell of thought was that a balance sheet took shape in Sim's mind about as follows:

For assets, he was alive; his strenuous bout of running had revived his circulation to warm and dry him; the floe was large and seemed solid; the contents of the boat's cuddy — the fresh-water breaker, the keg of ship's bread, the tight tin of matches, a knife, light lines and twine, a hatchet, a fetch bag with needles, palm, and a gub of oakum — had stayed put; the mast and sail, the long steering oar, the waif, and a spare iron had survived the wreck in fair condition; there would be no long, dark nights and it was the bearable season of the year.

For liabilities, he had a right arm and hand, the nerves and sinews of which had been strained and tortured "till they warn't no account then nor hain't been since," that shook and ached distractingly; summer ice was at best an uncertain support; the chances of rescue were a hundred to one, against; his supply of food was so scant and of such a nature that he could count on it for a few days only; he must constantly battle panic at thought of his future; he was haunted by his drowned crew and, at moments, almost beside himself as to the whereabouts of Cortes.

The summation of his situation, as he gave it, was: "When I'd totted up my chances, I seen my capital to get goin' on was jest about minus nothin'. This gave me a kind of a jolt in my midriff — but twarn't long till this wore off an' I begun to feel better. If yer hain't got nothin', yer can't lose much — an' I tell yer this is a real comfortin' thought in times o' trouble — so I set right out to forget what *might* happen, by raisin' a stir o' things to happen right *now.*"

And here it was evident that, together with his future, Sim jettisoned all account of time as it is reckoned in days and nights, hours and minutes; for, as he said, "there was a sight o' jobs that all oughter been done yesterday an' I got flustered

thinkin' how behind time I was; so as there warn't much difference between nighttime and daytime, I quit takin' any account
of it."

Here it took much questioning by the Skipper to draw from
Sim an account of his material achievements. To his intensely
practical mind it was evident that we would assume, for in-
stance, that his first job would be to "lash up a pung" from the
wreck of the boat, which would lift him and his stores above the
ice and snow — a base that could be moved and on which he
could eat, sleep, and "carry on with considerable comfort,"
when he had rigged a shelter cloth from part of the sail.

He refused to do more than mention the difficulty of this
accomplishment, handicapped as he was by the injury to his
right hand and the frequent interruptions of violent exercise to
keep his fingers and toes from "numbin'." He would not admit
that his patience must have been tried high or that, in the gusts
of discouragement that must have come to him, his fare of
hardtack washed down with a little water from the breaker and
as much snow as could be mingled with it gave little cheer or
satisfaction. We had finally to let our imaginations fill in the
gaps he left in his story until he described himself as "keepin'
house handy to the blasted carcass of a bull walrus that give me
plenty o' cheap meat — not *too* stinkin' — with the waif set up
solid an' flyin' good on the highest hummock o' the floe an' the
weather set fair an' warmish."

By further questioning, the Skipper pushed Sim to confess
that the discovery of the walrus came at the moment when he
was "losin' ambition" on the unvarying fare of hardtack and
water, with the further discouragement that only crumbs and
weevils were left in the bread barge. But he quickly qualified
this dismal picture by explaining the immediate renewal of his
strength by the change of diet and the systematic hunt he
instituted to fortify his situation further. The spare iron and a
club, split from the loggerhead of the boat, were his weapons;
anything that furnished meat, his quarry. And again his dogged

149

patience bore fruit, for he finally killed a seal, from which flowed comparative abundance.

In describing this incident, Sim became expansive. He told us how from the sealskin he cobbled a pair of shoepacks stuffed with oakum, a pair of drawers "to warm up my nether parts," and mittens that "was a comfort." All these made possible longer spells of sleep, an inexpressible luxury. With the oil tried out from the blubber — a pitifully small quantity at a time, in the match tin held over a feeble, tenderly guarded flame of shavings — he first "gaumed" the troublesome sores on his right arm and hand and then, of even more importance, fueled a cooking lamp "fixed up from the conch shell horn" as a font, with a braid of oakum for the wick. His gusto over the first whiff of fresh red meat a-broil made our mouths water; his house-keeping seemed a shade warmer and less dreary.

And then, just as I was pleasurably anticipating the climax of this saga — his delivery from the floe — Sim said, "But it warn't long after I got to havin' cooked vittles an' warm water till I woke up *stone-blind* — nothin' really but snow blindness, but I didn't know then there was such a complaint, an' with my eyes feelin' as if they was full o' sharp burrs I thought they was done for for all time, an' I ain't ashamed to say I took it hard."

How long he lay on the pung chewing the cud of despair he could not tell. Fortunately the horrors that took possession of his mind immobilized his body, until they were gradually dispelled by a cold, angry determination "to beat Fate an' go on livin'." Finally the orientation of his surroundings came uppermost and he began to plan the conduct of his new life in the dark.

His first move was to finger over the gear beside him until he had firm hold of the haft of the harpoon, which he so placed that it could be gripped by his knees as he knelt over it. Again by touch he found the harpoon line and worked it through his hand until the free end was reached. This he made fast to the pung. He then coiled the lines, turned the coil so that it might

150

run freely and, with the harpoon in his hand, started to crawl from his base in the direction he felt would bring him to the carcass of the walrus. With every faculty keyed to the highest pitch, he inched forward on this vitally important quest.

"An' by the steerin' of my immortal sweatin' soul," said he, "I fetched my landfall — an' I tell you when I struck onto it I felt sorter friendly to that old hunk o' meat. So I patted it all over to get the bearin's of it an' then druv my iron firm into his tough old neckpiece, hauled taut the line, an' there I was hitched up to home an' my vittles an' no chance to get lost between."

The impression that remains with me of this part of Sim's struggle for existence is one of aching sympathy. Life was so evidently a continuing round of torturingly minute activities, every one to be undertaken only after deep thought, with the execution so frequently failing through some unforeseen difficulty or accident. As an example, his routine was suddenly interrupted by the loss of his knife, an almost fatal disaster, through the unperceived fraying of the lanyard on which it was slung from his neck. By the time this happened he had extended his field of activities far beyond the territory between pung and walrus by making one end of a long line fast around his waist, with the other end hitched to the frame of the pung. So harnessed, he was able to explore safely his frozen surroundings in all directions within the limit of his tether; but in this case of the lost knife the wider freedom had complicated his search a thousandfold.

I was attacked by the "kinder holler feelin' " Sim said he had when he crawled away from the pung on this seemingly hopeless attempt to retrieve the knife. My solar plexus tied itself into a knot when, after uncounted time and myriad fumblings as he quartered over the rough, cold surface, he was forced back to his base by fatigue and the discouragement of failure; and when, as he lay spent and attempting to pump up his courage for another try, his hand, idly picked over the familiar objects that were so carefully ranged around his sleeping place, came suddenly on the knife enfolded in the loose strands of the gub of oakum, I, too, "broke out into a sweat o' thanksgivin'."

Then came the account of petty triumphs, depressing defeats, ingenious shifts, and amazing new aptitudes, while for the most part Sim sensed that the sun shone, torturing his sick eyes and, had he but thought of it, rotting the surface of the floe. As time passed, this weather, seemed also to soften Sim's practical caution. He became careless in the securing of his precious necessaries on and around the pung. More and more the obsession that Cortes was near at hand and in distress occupied his thoughts to set him wandering — on his feet, not a-crawl — restless and aimless, shouting and shouting till exhaustion forced him to return to his base to recuperate. It was during one of these wild, fruitless sallies that Fate almost landed a knockout.

"I'd been sleepin'," he explained, "when I come to sudden an' heard Cortes holler close by. I threw a clove hitch with the tether, 'round my waist; an' without botherin' to set it up solid with a half hitch, I started off to where it sounded as if the cuss must be. I figured I'd run out about thirty fathom o' line when, without any sort o' warnin', I soused down *under water*. When I come up I had to waste considerable time belchin' up what I'd swallered as I went down, for my silly mouth was open to call when I walked overboard. Then I had to fumble 'round to lay hold o' the ice, for I found it warn't no hole I'd gone into — and then I knowed what I'd oughter guessed if I'd been more reasonable: that the floe was breakin' up.

"When I finally found the ice, 'twas too thick to reach up to the top an' there warn't no shelves to get a handholt onto. This flustrated me some an' I hove on my tether in a hurry till I'd got all the slack down under me in a mess. By the time the line was taut an' I was jest startin' to put my weight on it, she come slack with a jerk an' down I went under agin. This time I didn't rise very good an' I knowed I was gettin' weak with cold.

"I was in a tight clinch an' I didn't see no way out; but then I figured I might as well drown kickin' as cryin', so I begun coastin' along the ice edge on the chanst there was a shelf somewheres — an' by damn if before I was froze solid I didn't come to a place where I could feel the floe was wore right down thin an' I could kinder wiggle onto it an' lay half afloat till I'd caught my breath. When I come to life a little I made a grab for my tether, but twarn't there; that slippery hitch o' mine had let go an' there I was in a tighter clinch 'n ever."

Here Sim stared hard at me, and after a moment's pause said:

"Bub! I want you to remember this: if ye can once get rid o' bein' afraid to die, you ain't goin' to have to go through the hell o' bein' scared to death every time ye get into a hole yer can't see no way out of. I got a firm grip o' this lesson that time out yander when I lost my tether, an' I hain't ever let go of it sence."

After this, perhaps because of the blurring of his impressions by spent vitality, Sim, in resuming his tale, responded grudgingly to the Skipper's frequent proddings for detail. Most of his answers were "Yes" or "No," with an occasional spurt of caustic explanation.

It was evident he took the blow of the loss of his tether literally lying down, but was fortunately soon stung into feverish activity by hail which drove on him before a heavy squall of cold wind. Exercise, vigorous enough to keep life in him, was now the primary concern; and fearing another fall overboard should he walk, he started crawling in the direction in which he believed his tether lay, trusting to one outstretched, groping hand to feel out the break in the ice and, if luck were with him, the rope. At first he went forward slowly, for again and again he had to stop to beat and chafe the circulation into numbing feet and hands. But suddenly the weather cleared, he felt the sun warm on his back — thawing him out — so that presently he was making good progress.

And then came the moment when he was convinced he had overrun his mark and was headed in the wrong direction. Feeling helpless and weak, he halted his crawl and sat upright. A fit of exasperation swept over him and he kicked and scuffled childishly — when in the height of his tantrum he felt a line catch on his left instep. Revived by this unbelievably good fortune, Sim, still on his hands and knees, made his way with speed to the pung, only to discover that it had been capsized. A feverish search further disclosed the loss of most of his carefully placed gear and precious stores. He had the answer to the sudden slackening of the tether when he had been in the water. He and the wind, combined with his own carelessness in neglecting to furl his weather cloth and lash down his other valuables, had succeeded in wrecking his stronghold.

Said Sim: "I was too damned discouraged an' tired to even die right then, so I followed up the line to the walrus an' slumped down in a heap on him — an' there I lay waitin' for the end!"

Followed by a pause, so long that I realized Sim considered the yarn had been spun to the last thread, while from my point of view there was still so much to be laid up that I finally burst out with: "But — but — how *did* you get off the floe and home again?"

"Oh, that," said he, "was all wrote out in the papers at Mazatlan when them Mexican sealers that come along before 'twas too late took me off the ice an' set me ashore there.

"I suspicion most of it was lies like all newspapers give out — but as there warn't much I can remember till I sort o' come to, an' figured I was aboard ship, fingerin' a blanket, it didn't make no odds what yarns them folks told. When I'd got a good holt o' the idea that I warn't layin' there on the ice, the sap begun to run in my mouth agin, an' I got considerable satisfaction thinkin' about the fish chowders to home on the Vineyard; an' when I felt a hand laid on my head an' heard a furrin voice sayin', 'You feel better, eh?' I managed to make that feller know

I was interested in some spoon vittles. Bean soup don't sound real hearty for a hungry man, but when I got a mug o' that inside me it set real good; an' I took a long caulk without nothin' on my mind.

"When I woke up it come over me slow that whenever I turned my head there was a square patch o' light in one quarter. Four or five times I turned my eyes away an' brought 'em back, an' every time there was that light — an' then I knew my eyes was better an' I warn't blind. Skipper, you ain't never felt so grateful for anything till you've lost it an' got it back agin! I tell you, when it soaked into me that I warn't totally blind, I jest laid there in my bunk for a spell with my toes an' fingers an' hair on my head squirmin' with happiness an' thanksgivin'.

"Twarn't long after that till I got about on my legs. The folks aboard that schooner was goodhearted, an' when I'd told the one who could talk some English about my eyes, he gave me a pair o' wooden spectacles with slits in 'em so I could see out in the sun, without gettin' stabbin' pains in my head. He told me the day they seen the waif flyin' on the floe it was calm an' they thought there might be some skins or somethin' with value layin' on the ice to be picked up for the trouble, so they launched a boat an' rowed over, an' I guess they was real disappointed when they only found a blasted walrus an' a man more dead than alive. Kind o' lucky for me though, warn't it?

"Their schooner was the *Sinaloa,* built to Mystic, Connecticut — very moderate in a breeze but a good ghoster."

TWELVE

Dicey Comes Ashore

A S SIM brought his saga to a close I felt strangely content to bask in the warm sunshine flooding that hilltop where we sat. A few moments of silence followed as the Skipper, staring at his feet, chewed a broad stalk of this spring's green grass, while Sim fixed his eyes on the distant view off to the northeast, where the rolling hills and sandy beaches of Martha's Vineyard shimmered through miles of blue haze. Watching Sim's motionless face — craggy and seamed by its rough encounters with Nature at her fiercest — I thought (reversing the description of the schooner *Sinaloa*), "What a performer in a breeze, even though a trifle moderate in a calm." And as I watched, the faraway look in the blue eyes veered to one of tenderness as the two little sails of Jethro's boat, standing in for the anchorage, broke into the line of vision.

"Time to be headin' fer home," said Sim, getting to his feet and starting off over the rough, grassy hillside, presently to pick up the footpath by which we'd come across the Island.

Without seeming to hurry, he led at a pace on the return journey that forced the Skipper and me to set all sail to stay with him. There was no loitering by the way this time, and while the grade was, on the whole, downhill, I felt before we came to the landing place as if the tilt of the Island had been reversed. As we struck the beach, Sim kicked off his top-boots and, rolling his trouser legs above his knees, waded out to steady the bow of Jethro's boat as it nosed onto the sand. Within a minute Jethro had jerked the two sprits out of their beckets and furled the sails by frapping them 'round the masts with some turns of the sheets and splashed ashore in his gum boots and oilskin overalls.

Well above high-water mark, and in line with the boat, stood a wooden capstan anchored to a deadman driven deep in the sand. There was a heavy fall and tackle hooked to the deadman and a pile of light, greased skids lying off to one side. While the Skipper and I lent a hand, Jethro laid a track of skids from the capstan down to the boat, shoved a heavy iron bolt through a hole bored low in the stem, clapped on a strop, stretched the tackle, hooked the free block into the strop, took three turns of the fall around the capstan drum, and with Sim still standing by the bow and the Skipper overhauling the slack of the fall, Jethro and I started the drum a-turning by pushing on opposite ends of the long capstan bar, so that presently the heavy boat slid up the beach to be berthed high and dry within a few steps of a wooden shed called the "fish house."

" 'Tain't no trick at all if you've got the gear," said Jethro to me as he tossed a dozen or so big splint baskets from the fish house to Sim, who had climbed aboard the boat. Within a few minutes these baskets were back in the shed loaded with clean run cod, mottled green and brown and averaging twelve to fifteen pounds apiece.

"What'll they tally, Father?" asked Jethro as he gaffed a fish and slapped it down on a long bench under the window.

"About three quintal," answered Sim, running his eye over the baskets, while he tested the edge of a knife on his thumbnail.

"Well, you pick out a prime one and run up to the house and help Dicey fix dinner," said Jethro. "Fried cod steaks and mashed turnip 'guess'll do — and tell Dicey to fetch them two chairs out o' Norton's."

And as Sim, like an obedient child, chose a fine fish and started out of the door with our dinner dangling by gill and eye from the thumb and forefinger of his left hand, Jethro commenced to operate on the cod lying on the bench.

For an hour or more sitting on upturned tubs the Skipper and I watched a succession of big fish pass under Jethro's skillful hands, which moved with the precision of machinery and so fast that at times there seemed to be four of them instead of two, the whole performance punctuated by the snicking of the knife, the plop of livers and tongues as they dropped into their respective kegs, the faint crackle of the "sounds" as they were ripped out, the rasp of coarse salt rubbed into spread belly-cavities, and finally the squelch of dressed fish pressed home into a barrel of brine.

At first, as he was getting his hand in, Jethro was silent. Then without looking up from his work he said:

"I guess Father sprung his yarn about livin' on the floe off the Northwest Coast, didn't he?" and without waiting for any reply he continued: "Some folks think his headpiece ain't caulked real tight — but I'd rather take his judgment on most matters that count, than any man's I've met up with yet. And when it comes to a pinch, that left arm and hand o' hisn is wuth more'n a dozen. I owe my bein' here to that judgment and that arm; and some others, includin' my wife, does, too. I don't remember seein' you, Skipper, to talk with since Dicey and me was married, three year ago come this fall — and I don't figure you've heard the straight of that October night and early mornin' when Dicey come ashore in these parts. There's the Mornin' Mercury's account of it, tucked under the shingle that's tacked onto the inside of the door yonder along with my tally sheets. You and your young friend take and read it over, and then I'll tell ye where the feller that wrote it got off soundin's. What he didn't know about salt water doin's was a caution!"

Jumping up from my seat I ran over to the door to find a folded yellowed sheet of newspaper, which I handed to the Skipper. Glancing at it he returned it to me, saying:

"Read it yourself; I had my go with it at home the day it was published."

So, sitting down again, I went to work on the two columns of fine print under the caption: "British Ship Wrecked on Cuttyhunk."

Like so many reports of such events, this account emphasized the loss of life that had occurred but failed to explain the conditions and details responsible for the tragedy. When I'd come to the end I had a confused impression of "howling storm . . . raging seas . . . overturned lifeboat" and eventual rescue of a "pitiful remnant" of the crews of both boat and ship.

As I looked up from my reading, the Skipper said: "Now, Jethro — the road's clear, so let her go!"

"Well, Skipper, so's your friend, who I presume ain't very well acquainted here, will understand how we was all placed, I'll say that Mother'd died over on the Vineyard the spring before; and Father bein' lonesome, I'd fetched him to Cuttyhunk where I was actin' captain of the gov'ment lifesavin' station — to hearten him up and keep an eye on him. He boarded to Veeder's up on the hill, lendin' a hand with this and that and gettin' along pretty good, all things considered.

"September'd been rough and foggy, with three strandin's — two schooners and one tern — keepin' us busy and, what's more, bothered by that Humane Society's lifeboat, manned by volunteer Cuttyhunkers tryin' to get ahead of us and take the credit for what was done. I tell you, Skipper! It ain't no bed o' roses to handle a gov'ment job such as mine was there when an outfit like that old Society — the first folks to organize lifesavin' on this coast — feels their holt on the business slippin'. You can't blame them boys with their boat tryin' all they knowed how to get to wind'ard of us regular paid hands — they feelin' that they was up against Uncle Sam with unlimited money and gear behind him. It's just human nature to be galled and reckless-mad, and Father he'd figured there'd be an accident 'fore long if somethin' warn't done to sweeten up that sour mess o' bad blood. Me and my crew down to the station was about as popular as a skunk to a church picnic, which ain't a healthy arrangement on an island with half a hundred folks livin' together, and some of 'em oath-bound to save the lives and property of shipwrecked strangers. It warn't only the weather and the tides and the fogs we was up against, but all the folks on Cuttyhunk, too, schemin' to give us a black eye and put us in wrong with the public.

"Come October the weather set fair and stayed that way right through, so's all we had to do was to keep patrol, overhaul gear, and put on a couple o' practice drills with the boats. Come sunup the twenty-third, there was a moderate northerly breeze with quite a fleet o' colliers flyin' light and a four-master with lumber runnin' out o' the Sound to west'ard on the last half o' the ebb. As pretty a mornin' as you'd ever see that time o' year. Come noon there was considerable traffic workin' to east'ard on the flood. Along towards four in the afternoon a swell begun to heave in from the south'ard and it growed fast. Then just before sundown here come a little brig-rigged vessel alone, from east'ard, creepin' along on the first o' the ebb. I got my glass on her and seen she was British by her rig and build, and I says to myself, 'What's that stranger doin' in the mouth o' the Sound this time o' day, with the breeze likely to peter out, the sea makin' up, and the tide changin' to flood come midnight?' Then I ketched sight of a woman on her deck; and I don't know why — but I got real uneasy.

160

"From then 'til six o'clock, supper time, I was busy writin' up my log, and such, in the station and took no account o' the weather. Whilst we was at table I heard the shingle, south side o' the Neck, begin to scream in the undertow after every swoosh of a breaker; so I went outside to have a look around. 'Twas oily calm; not a breath stirrin' and gettin' cold. A three-quarters moon was pokin' up, bright as a new dollar, over Gay Head, and them swells with broad lanes o' moonshine runnin' crisscross over their tops was comin' on like hills — silent as death 'til they tripped on bottom and burst. It beat any Fourth o' July fireworks.

"In ten minutes I was back again indoors, so's I could get the first night patrol's report myself when he'd turn it in over the wire from the West End lookout station.

"When his voice come through I says without waitin', 'How's that brig layin'?' and he says, 'By Jesus, Cap'n, I can't see her half the time, nor the lightship neither. The seas out here's biggern' I ever seen 'em — and not a sigh of a breeze. But I figger the brig's about abreast the lightship and layin' head to the south'ard. She must be catchin' it wicked with the ebb runnin' against them rollers!'

"And I says: 'You stay where you be and report every half-hour!'

"I hadn't no more'n hung up when Father come in, and I seen he was set on some notion — the whites o' his eyes was bloodshot, and I knowed he meant business. He jerked his head at the door — so we went outside and down the beach a piece, where we could be alone.

" 'Son,' says he — and he never calls me son unless he's real worked up — 'that brig'll come ashore about two hours after turn o' tide an' nothin' we can do'll save her. There ain't a tug to Bedford could face that rip tonight, much less get a line aboard her, an' we can't tow her with the boats even if *we* could get alongside, which we can't do 'til the flood's runnin' — an' then it'll be too late! I've been watchin' how things was out to the west end, an' them seas is breakin' a mile 'most, outside Sow an' Pigs, an' as I come back along the north shore there was acres o' broken water all between here an' Hen an' Chickens — on Ribbon Reef an' them three-fathom knolls to the north'ard. You can hear the roar of it easy from the beach across the Pond. Now here's what'll happen: them boys in the Humane Boat'll launch under the lighthouse — an' I reckon they can just about get off the beach there. Then they'll pull out an' lay so if the brig comes ashore they'll have the jump on ye.

" 'But you an' me an' two o' your boats is goin' to be out in that neighborhood ourselves. An' whilst you may be *a* captain in gov'ment service, I'm *the* Captain o' this outfit from now on 'til this night's over — an' don't you make no mistake about that!'

"Well, Skipper, when you've had a father like Sim as long as I have, there come times when you feel and act as if you was nothin' but a boy again. So I says:

" 'Heave away! The deck's yourn! But I'm the Mate, and orders goes through *me;* and don't *you* make no mistake about *that!'*

"And I will say, when he'd finished spillin' what was on his mind, there warn't nothin' overlooked or left to chance, as far as I could figure; and within the hour we'd launched from the north beach, abreast the station — where it was moderate quiet — with Father in charge of the whaleboat with four hands to the oars; me in the lifeboat with a full crew — and my mate up to the West End lookout, all primed for signalin'."

At this point Jethro paused in his narrative to shift brine barrels, and when he was back at the bench with fish passing through his hands again he continued silent for some time. At last he laid down his knife and turned to face us, saying:

"And there you have it, Skipper, just the way it was — bright moonlight, ungodly sea, and dead calm — with everything happening the way Father foretold. There's spells a man has to go through, that he can't hardly keep clear in his mind after

162

they're over; and what come that night and early mornin's one of 'em, 's far's I'm concerned. To tell the truth I don't hanker, and never have, to try to figure step by step all we done. Fust place 'twould take too long to tell, and second, 'twould sound as if I was tootin' the Gofford horn kind o' loud. All any folks that warn't there needs to know is, the brig struck about two o'clock in the mornin' and we was layin' where we could see her ridin' in on one o' them rollers all lit up for a flash, by the moon. Then she disappeared in a lather o' foam and spray, and presently — sharp as a pistol shot — above the roar o' the breakin' seas, here come a crack, and a weak, pitiful cry as she fetched up on the rocks — the lonesomest sight and sound I 'most ever seen or heard. And we as near as that, and yet too far to do more than burn flares to let them strangers know we'd seen 'em and was standin' by.

"Come false dawn, and them ambitious boys aboard the Humane Boat begun to pull out for the wreck — Father and me trailin' 'em as agreed. Then the moon dipped, the sky filmed, and 'twas darker'n the inside of a tar barrel and I sensed by the feel o' the helm we was in broken water where the back run o' the rollers was ketchin' on shoal spots inside the reef. Another minute, and Father's boat showed a red flare — and I knowed them youngsters in the Society's boat had come to grief up ahead. So we quit pullin' and layed. Ten minutes more and Father touched off a blue light and we begun to pull easy — headed for the Island — cruisin', with our eyes and ears open for what we might run across.

"Between then and dawn the whaleboat got one — alive — out o' that capsized boat, and I got two that warn't — the sea and rocks had got to 'em first. We just drove onto 'em and hauled what there was aboard; and I thought of them poor folks on the brig — if she was still there, which I misdoubted.

"I reckon 'twas past five, with the stars palin' fast, when Father touched off another blue light and we headed out again with the ebb commencin' to cock up them seas and Father's flare bobbin' into sight now and then between us and the reef. 'Twas chancy work — pull for all you was worth a few strokes, then hold her steady whilst you rode one that looked like breakin', and me sweatin' more and more to sight the wreck. At last when we was on top of a long one, I saw a lower mast stickin' up out of a welter o' broken water with a huddle o' folks in the top. When we come up again, 'twas gone, and there was the whaleboat ridin' on her tail on the face of a sea just dimplin' and edgin' to break.

"And now, Skipper, I can't say much more — except, some time later, when 'twas light enough for the water to begin to blue just before sunup, there come that spar with two folks still in the top — stabbin' out through the body of a snorer bearin' down on us. And as we rose to it, that mast was hove by us and I seen that woman — Dicey — just out o' reach; and I done what no man callin' himself a seaman had oughter do. For I kicked off my boots and everything down to drawers, singlet, and clasp knife on a lanyard, and went outboard. 'Twas desertion o' my sworn duty and but for Father it might ha' cost the lives o' my crew — let alone my own, Dicey's, and the old man's with her.

"When I laid hold o' that top I found them two was lashed to it, without a kick o' their own left in 'em. 'Twas ticklish business hangin' on — that spar didn't lay flat; more up and down; liftin' me once or twice nigh out o' water. Three times my boat come up abreast, and me with my knife ready to slash them lashin's. And three times that stick of ourn bobbed out o' reach. Then here come Father in the whaleboat, handlin' her with gloves, and I cut — and as I done so I caught a crack on my head from some bit o' loose gear. When I come to, there was Dicey and the old man layin' in the whaler, with Father still at the steerin' oar, his face set grim. When I opened my eyes again he gave me one look, and I felt small and ord'nary — just the way when he'd found me playin' the fool, to home, old days on the

Vineyard. But there warn't a word out o' him 'til I was abed that afternoon in the station. Then all he says, was:

" 'Jethro, you lay there 'til your headpiece is mended; an' then you throw up this job here — you ain't fit to be responsible for gov'ment property. The woman's comin' on good, an' her uncle too — if that's any consolation to ye.'

"And so, a few days later, when I got my legs under me, I wrote out my resignation and mailed it to headquarters; though there warn't no blame attachin' to me then or after, when the hearin' was held. And here's a funny thing, Skipper, I've noticed about some folks — the more they think they're under obligations to ye, the more they keep away from ye and act up mean. All the time we was waitin' 'round for the hearin' to be held, Cap'n Stillwell made himself scarce where I was, so's I got the notion he was figurin' to get his knife into me when he come to say his piece. And Father, he didn't say nothin' to help; just mooned around mum as an oyster 'til I felt I was branded — the man responsible for all them that had been drowned. If it hadn't been for that stranger, Dicey, I don't know as I could've stuck them days without losin' my grip.

"But she stood by through all that bad time — showin' all she knowed how that she believed I'd done right when she and her uncle was adrift on that spar. It warn't so much what she said the two or three times we was together — for to tell the truth, I couldn't rightly understand her lingo then, or she mine — as 'twas the way she looked and behaved to hearten me up. And I made out somehow that she give Father and me the credit for her bein' alive. I managed to get it clear she was an orphan and had come on this cruise with her uncle to get shut of a stepmother she couldn't gee with, after her father'd died.

"But when the day come and we was all up before the investigatin' board, I found Dicey's uncle was about as good a friend to me and Father as we could've had. For he brought it out when his turn come, that bein' a stranger to this coast, he'd miscalculated the set o' the tides in the mouth o' the Sound, and

165

by the time the breeze dropped and he seen he was in for trouble, there warn't any man, includin' me, could done more'n we did.

"He said when the flood tide begun to set the brig to north-'ard towards the reef, he let go both anchors in hopes she'd fetch up and lay; but soon's the cables come taut they ripped out the windlass and she commenced to drag, and it warn't long before the cables cut down the hawse pipes — so's she was sinkin' 'fore she struck. After the talk was all over, I got a clean bill o' health; but with all them fine Cuttyhunk boys and the brig's crew gone, and with Father's opinion o' me, I didn't hanker to stay 'round the Island no longer.

"A couple o' weeks more and Cap'n Stillwell had fixed to go home to Scarborough, and Dicey — well, she'd fixed to stay in these parts with me and Father; and so when the day for movin' come, the four of us crossed over to Bedford, and Dicey and me was married, and we bid Cap'n Stillwell goodbye. And I ain't ashamed to say I was considerably sorry to see the last o' the old man, even if he was a Britisher. That winter we boarded to Vineyard Haven, and come here the spring follerin', and — "

Suddenly a soft, caressing voice broke in on Jethro's clipped, nasal twang, asking:

"That'll coom to tha dinner now, lad?" And there, facing us in the doorway, stood Juno, or better, soft-eyed Athene, with a baby in the crook of one arm and a toddler clinging to her skirt.

"Now, Dicey," said Jethro, "you fetch these friends o' mine up to the house whilst I finish dressin' down. 'Twon't take more'n two shakes of a lamb's tail."

THIRTEEN

Island Queen

TWO YEARS after my first visit to Noman's Land, the Skipper and I were making another short cruise on my little ketch-rigged *Fox*. About three o'clock of a sultry August afternoon, with the help of a languid southerly breeze and the last pulse of a flood tide, we'd succeeded in laying up close enough along the beach on the north side of the neck to work into the pond at Cuttyhunk.

After getting the anchor down and the sails furled we felt uncomfortably hot and oppressed, lying as we did in the lee of the highland under a sun which glowed like a blob of red-hot iron in a thickening gloom of heat-haze to the west. Said the Skipper:

"How about stretching our legs ashore on the weather side of the Island, where this paltry air may be a bit cooler and more vigorous than it is here?"

"Just the chance to pick up a bit of worthwhile wreckage among the boulders on the South Beach," thought I, as I jumped to cast off the fasts of the *Peapod,* which lay bottom up over the skylight, and presently to drop her, bottom down, alongside, with a resounding spank as she hit the water.

An hour later we were lying prone on a big flat-topped rock at the foot of a sheer seventy-foot bank of moraine, down which we'd slithered from a footpath that meandered along the ragged brow of the high bluffs marking the southwesterly shore of the Island. As one after another long, glassy swells rolling in from the ocean reared up just before toppling over to break among the boulders and shingle, their crests were ruffled by puffs of the gentle breeze running over them. A second later these puffs, cooled and salted by the spray picked up from the breakers, were easing us of our burden of heat and toil. Even the slight distress aroused by the sight of several stranded and shattered hulks lying along the beach was soothed by the splash of water; and we were content, so that I, for one, fell asleep.

But there must have come a puff strong enough to flutter the brim of my hat, which waked me. Idly I stared out over the endless lines of swells heaving themselves ashore. Suddenly I saw a shaggy, shapeless bundle roll up on the face of a wave about to break, and in another moment come riding in on a smother of foam to the foot of our rock, where it stuck fast in the rift of a flanking boulder. Here might be the treasure I hoped to find! I scrambled from my perch and was soon pawing over this tangle of flotsam.

I found that the foundation of the snarl of rockweed and frayed rope ends was a smashed, splintered section of light boat-planking and timbers with traces of white paint showing here and there under a crust of barnacles. As I ripped off handfuls of the clinging seaweed any hope of finding a prize faded, and I was about to give over my search when I uncovered a black, knee-high rubber boot jammed between a plank and timber. The condition of the boot seemed so good that I pried it loose and held it, sole up, to rid it of water. After the first gush I shook the boot to be sure the last drop was out, and heard a slight rattle. Then I gave it a more vigorous shake —

when, to my horror, out slid the shank and foot bones of a human leg, to lie at my feet, picked clean and chalky white.

Too startled to cry out, I instinctively held up the empty boot toward the Skipper on the rock above me. Some spark of my emotion must have struck him, for a moment later he was beside me, staring down at the evidence of tragedy so unexpectedly revealed. And then, without a word, we both set to work to discover some clue which might lead to the identity of these remains.

As there was no mark other than the maker's, inside or out, on the boot, we dropped it and commenced, bit by bit, to clear the weed and barnacles from the raffle of planking and timbers. All at once the Skipper exclaimed, "What do you make of this?" as he pointed to some dabs of black paint on a section of plank he'd been carefully scraping with the point of his knife. Little by little the flecks of black resolved themselves into the disjointed but unmistakable letters — "U-M-A-."

"Uma" — I repeated it over and over several times without comprehension, and then, in a flash, I caught it. "Humane" — the lifeboat of the Humane Society which had capsized one October night, drowning most of her crew — the night which Jethro Gifford, as we sat in the fish house on Noman's, had so vividly described, "dead calm with an ungodly sea," when the British brig had stranded and broken up on Sow and Pigs reef. It was all clear to us now — these shattered bones were all that was left of "one o' them fine young Cuttyhunkers."

For a little while we both stood silent, reviewing this dark chapter of accident, until those few fragments of bone, lying pitiful and forlorn at our feet, stirred us to gather them reverently and carry them and the boot to a nook in the shelter of the bluff, where we buried them deep in sandy loam above highwater mark and built a cairn over their grave.

Sobered by the afternoon's experience, I boarded the *Fox* again with an urge stirring in me to visit Noman's without delay, to tell the Gifford family all that had happened here on the beach. By the time supper was over this urge had grown so insistent that I asked the Skipper:

"Do you think tonight's a good chance to get over to Noman's, for another day there?"

"Fair enough — if, after we've rounded the lightship, you're agreeable to my turning in for the rest of the night," was his reply.

And so it came about that shortly after midnight I was alone on deck while the *Fox*, her sails asleep and dew drenched, was making silent but steady headway to the southwest over the long swells, their tops still ruffled by the enduring southerly breeze.

When the first silvery light of dawn began to gray the sea, I was amazed that my long night watch had come to an end. It was incredible that the dark, lonely hours had been sped so quickly by my puzzlement as to how that boot and its identifying evidence had been steered to my hands by the mysterious pilotage of time, tide, wind, and water, after lying hid for months in some rock-locked cranny. It had all been beyond the realm of reason — not worth the attempt of solution — and yet, inasmuch as I had been freed from the usual battle with drowsiness, I was grateful to this riddle of the sea.

Later, when the sun broke the horizon line to the southeast, two little sails of a boat — black against the red-gold light — nicked the glowing disk. I rapped on the scuttle slide to call the Skipper on deck to share the scene.

Other than those distant sails there was no sign of life or land out here on the ocean, for the northeast quadrant of the sky where Noman's and Martha's Vineyard should have shown was shrouded by a pall of dark blue haze. The *Fox* seemed very small and far from home. I shoved the tiller down to bring her 'round onto the starboard tack, convergent with the course of the other boat. A moment later she, too, had changed her course and was running downwind to meet us.

As if seeking companionship in their loneliness, the two boats slowly closed the distance. A half-hour later they were alongside each other, fifty feet apart — and we on the *Fox* were gamming with Jethro and Sim; for it was their double-sprit rigged "Island boat," of all others, we had met up with that morning.

After inquiries as to health and codfish, the Skipper said: "Look here, Jethro, I wish you'd take this boy of mine aboard your boat to help tend trawl today and lend me Sim to pilot the *Fox* into Noman's — where we'll expect you later and lend you a hand with your day's fare. I'll guarantee he's no Jonah, and I'll bet you a good cigar he'll bring you beginner's luck."

"Well" — after a little pause — boomed Jethro, "ef he ain't too finicky about gettin' mussed up and sore hands and lame back, I'll do it — just to pleasure you, Skipper, you understand." And thereat he let draw his foresail, which had been aback, and getting way on his boat, wore her around under our stern, from where she forged slowly alongside, her sails ashake in the eye of the wind, so that "it warn't no trick at all," as Sim expressed it, for him and me to swap places. A minute more and the two boats had drawn apart, the *Fox* reaching away to the northeast, while the *Islander* was again standing close-hauled to the southwest.

For a few minutes, as we edged slowly to windward, Jethro was so absorbed in searching the horizon ahead that, although I was eager to tell my tale of the boot, I held my tongue and put in the time "learning the ropes" of the *Islander.*

Like my *Fox,* she was a double-ender, carvel built; but there all resemblance ceased. About eighteen feet overall, she was of light draft — two-feet-six — and light construction, with a beam of nearly seven feet. Flat floored and hard bilged, she was open from stem to stern except for a small section of deck at the after end, on which was mounted a horse of wrought iron so shaped as to allow the tiller full play beneath. Under the deck was a locker. The foremast was stepped in the "eyes" of her, the forward thwart forming a partner. There was a midship thwart, and three feet aft of it another thwart through which the mainmast stepped. Both sails were spritsails, the fore loose-footed, the main with a very light boom. The foresail was rigged with double sheets rendering around stout oak pegs under the rail, and when close-hauled overlapped the mainmast. The main sheet rendered through a block on the iron horse and a bull's-eye on the boom. The gunwales were topped by waterways and washboard. There was a noticeable absence of smith-work and nonessential gear; but in every line and fitting she proclaimed herself a development of environment and special purpose.

As I noted these details from fore to aft, my eyes finally came to Jethro where he stood in the stern, his left hand on the tiller and the lee foresheet in his right. As I watched his big-boned, hairless face, the color and texture of old ivory, his gray eyes suddenly shifted from their intent searching, to meet mine with a quizzical twinkle as he asked:

"Think you've got the hang of her while I was pickin' up them trawl buoys? Runnin' down wind to meet you folks kinder throwed me off my course, so't I misdoubted we'd have some fumblin' 'round to raise 'em. I'll bet a dollar to a dime you can't spot 'em yet for fifteen minutes by the watch."

And he was right; for, search the horizon and the sparkling sea as intently as I might, twenty minutes passed before two little black flags, a long distance apart, bobbed and fluttered into sight on the shoulders of long swells, to disappear again in the succeeding valleys.

Steadily but slowly we worked up to the weathermost flag, which was flying from the top of a long, limber spruce sapling lashed to a tight-headed, ballasted keg afloat at the end of a light anchor-roding. Approaching this buoy and marker from to leeward, Jethro chose a moment, with nice judgment of pace and distance, to shoot the *Islander* into the wind so that, as I stood forward in the bows, I could hook onto the

roding with a short-handled fish gaff just as she lost all headway, while Jethro slipped the sprits out of their beckets and
furled the sails.

"Weigh that killick and get it aboard without snarlin' the
trawl more'n you can help," directed Jethro as he came forward beside me to fit an open-jawed iron roller, like an over-
sized rowlock, into a socket on the starboard washboard.

Hand over hand I hauled up about twenty fathom of roding,
until the killick — a three-pronged crotch cut from an upper
branch of an oak, in the fork of which was jammed and lashed a
twenty-pound, smooth beach pebble — appeared, with the
end of a heavy, tarred "ground line" bent to a becket in the
crown. While I leaned overside to lift inboard this homemade
but efficient anchor, Jethro twitched out the bend knot, rove the
ground line to the roller, and commenced overhauling trawl.

Presently up came the first ganging — a three-foot length of
cod line bent to the trawl — and on the free end of it a well-
hooked, goggle-eyed cod which Jethro landed in the waist of
the boat with a swift twitch and slat on the rail.

"Jump aft," he ordered, "and strip off them good clothes o'
yourn and stow 'em in the locker, where you'll find Father's
apron — I guess you'll have to reef it some — and haul trawl
while I coil down."

A moment later, wrapped in a great pinafore of tarpaulin
which hung nearly to my ankles in spite of a lanyard tight
around my waist to hitch it up, I joined Jethro in the bows and
took over the trawl from him as he went aft and commenced
coiling the ground line and gangings in one of six empty tubs
which lay in the stern sheets.

For a while the hauling of line over the roller seemed light
work, and although I made a bungling job of slatting fish off
taken hooks, enough blank gangings came inboard to encourage me to feel I was getting on. But when for a spell all the
gangings, with only a fathom interval between them, came up
loaded each with a big fish which I had to stun with the muckle

173

(a short, heavy club of oak) before swinging it aboard, or with a series of "scrubs" (whatever was not cod) which had to be dealt with overside, I felt I'd tackled a more hopeless task than Hercules in the Augean stables. That trawl, sagging far ahead of us and arced out to the south by the strong ebb tide, looked interminable, while the speck of black flag marking its end seemed, as it actually was, miles away. For this trawl was a night-set, full-length one — six tubs with ten skates, sixty fathoms to the tub, a total of thirty-six hundred fathoms — a lot of gear to handle on one tide! And to add to my sense of hopelessness there were signs of wear and tear on my hands already; while, besides its aching muscles, my back crisped at the thought of Jethro's tolerant but scornful eyes as he watched me fumbling with my part of the work. But, at the very moment when I felt I'd have to throw up my hands and quit, Jethro said quietly:

"Easy does it, young feller — ain't no call to bust yer biler thinkin' of all them fish ahead — if they're hooked, there they be and a minute more or less won't hurt none."

So encouraged, I calmed down and began to learn the rhythm of the business. And finally, when I'd caught my second wind, a hope began to stir that I might hold out to the finish. But, by the Lord Harry! That was a long trawl before I'd come to the end of it and hauled aboard the keg buoy and killick; and although there were several long stretches where ganging after ganging came up barren, I had to admit, as the Duke of Wellington did after Waterloo, that my staying the course had been a "damned close-run thing."

Without lifting a finger to help, I watched Jethro spread a light tarpaulin over our fare, and then, too breathless and worn out to speak, I slumped down on top of it.

For a few minutes my raw palms throbbed, the small of my back ached like a tooth, and I was wide awake with misery. But I suspect 'twas not long before that night watch of mine, together with the hot sun, was too much even for pain; for the next thing I was aware of was fetching up with a jolt against the lee washboard, as the boat lay down to the strong breeze coming from off the bluffs on the north shore of Noman's. Twenty minutes later, with sails furled and the centerboard housed in its trunk, the *Islander* was nosing onto the white sand of the landing beach, where Sim stood in water up to his knees prepared to steady the bow as it grounded, while farther up on dry land was the Skipper, with shirt sleeves rolled up ready for action. As we slowed to a stop Jethro went over the side in his gum boots and oilskins and splashed ashore, while I followed. The cool, clear water surging up to my waist under Sim's apron was most refreshing.

"Well, now, Skipper," said Jethro, "Supposin' your young friend — who I'll say done pretty good this mornin' — gets washed up down to the beach, and his clothes on, and then both of ye stroll up to the house while Father and me dress down and get these fish into pickle. I know Dicey'll be real glad to see ye. There hain't been too much company 'round since the last o' the folks that lived here went ashore for good, a year ago come next month."

I jumped at this proposal, for, much as I enjoy fish and fishing, I'd had enough of 'em for one day. And as I sat in the shallows getting clean, the sting of the salt water in my raw palms heightened my respect and admiration for Sim and Jethro, who, day after day, dressed and cured fish, straightened and baited those countless soft hooks, laid out those miles of trawl without kink or snarl, and then, rousing out before dawn, sailed forth again to sweat up interminable fathoms of harsh line — all to the end that they might earn food and sleep enough to repeat this round of back-breaking labor. "A hard, hard life!" I thought; but before that day was over I had an inkling of the compensations — liberty, and independence — that they enjoyed.

Freed from the taint of codfish and clothed in accustomed garments, with no immediate call for unusual exertion, and with the prospect of dinner not too distant, I felt my lot to be a happy one in this, the best of all worlds. It was in such mood after my bath that I joined the Skipper for our stroll up to the house.

A few steps beyond the western end of the landing beach we came to a little footpath which led up to the bluffs. As we topped the sharp rise, there sprang into sight, just as I recalled it, the huddle of ten or twelve small gray cabins clustered round a larger building painted white. Some impulse — perhaps the ardor of the sun — caused us to halt and look out toward the northwest, where across miles of glinting sea the highlands of Cuttyhunk broke the horizon — a faint blur on the soft blue of the sky. Suddenly a spasm of loneliness swept over me at the thought that to the southeast of us there was no land nearer than Africa. And when the Skipper exclaimed, "Lord! think of standing here alone in a winter nor'wester!" I felt helplessly enmeshed by the immensity of ocean surrounding us. When we started walking again I kept my eyes down on that narrow path traced by men's feet. I felt it to be the one thin thread linking me to human affairs.

As we came among the houses I looked up and about, only to feel more forlorn; for, with the exception of one where a chimney smoked, it was evident all were tenantless. But it was the doors and windows, staring vacantly without stir of life behind them, even more than the mold of neglect, and the disrepair, which drove home the realization that here lay the unburied corpse of a community. My empty stomach turned over as, gazing at these silent and forsaken dwellings, the picture of the black boot and shattered, white bones came vividly to mind. It was a bit too thick! I wished I'd never come here! And the Skipper, when I glanced at his face, showed that he too was deeply moved by this pitiable sight.

It was the sharp slam of a door — the door of the house with the smoking chimney — that broke the current of our thoughts, switching them from shadow to sunshine as the splendid figure of Dicey — or "Boadicea," as I could only think of her — came toward us. In her arms she held, as before, a tiny baby, while at her knee little Viola clung to her skirt. Her greeting as we met left no doubt that she was "real pleased" to see us. It was needless to be solicitous about her health, or that of the children — it could not have been topped by Hygeia herself. But as we stood there admiring the baby a fat little hand was poked out appealingly toward the Skipper, to which he responded by gently taking hold of the fairy-like fingers, as he asked the mother:

"Don't you ever feel lonely, 'way off here, Boadicea? And how about the doctor when this newcomer arrived?"

Pausing a moment as if to grasp the significance of the question, Boadicea looked at the Skipper with an expression almost of pity in her dark eyes, while the shadow of a smile curved her lips.

"Nay, sir," said she at last in her deep, lazy voice. "Wi' a man like mine and wi' all God's clean air to breathe, a' could niver be lone-like here. And as for th'on doctor, a've had a good laugh to mysen when a' thought on't. He was to coom on a Thursda', an' Jess coomed a Thursda', to be sure, but a Thursda' a fortni't afore her time. So when t' great man stepped ashore a' bided in t'hoose, an' when 'e rapped on t'door a' opened to 'im wi' Jess on ma arm an' a' says, 'Tha's coom ower late, man, dear, an' tha mun turn aboot an' go hoam' — an' a' made as if to shut t'door in's face.

"But Jethro gi'ed 'im t' brass for 'is trouble, an' bid 'im to dinner. An' when a'd showed 'im Jess an' tell't 'im how knowin' an' gentle Father were when her coomed, 'e says playful-like, 'ed'd have t' law on us for robbin' 'im of 'is practice. 'E wouldna' stay th' night, but 'e left me a boax wi' pins an' clouts a' could do wi' for t' young-uns."

This expression of Boadicea's satisfaction with life — so conclusive and undebatable — had the effect of contracting the encircling miles of sea and dispelling the eeriness of those blank, staring doors and windows. And when the Skipper had said, "You deserve a crown for your courage, Boadicea," her laugh and blush banished every vestige of our gloom. Here was boundless life triumphing over eternal death. How dared we be dispirited?

Looking up at the sun, our hostess said: "A'm thinkin' you'll be hungerin' soon, so a' mun go hoam to ma' business," and with that she shifted Jess from her own to the Skipper's arms, and after putting Viola's hand in mine she marched off, to enter one of the houses where a half-open door sagged on its hinges. A minute later she came out with two heavy wooden chairs — mere feathers, as she handled them — to lead the way to her own quarters. Presently we crossed the threshold to come directly into a low-studded room.

Now that every trace of that house is gone, I am aware how greatly a dwelling of its sort would be prized had it been preserved. For inasmuch as it was the last of its kind to shelter a family maintaining itself by shore fishing on Noman's, it would have been a unique example of an unrecorded, little-known, and long since vanished way of life in New England.

Like many of the old houses in the stranded port of Rye, in Sussex, this one was diminutive but massive; for its frame was of big ship's timbers and knees — flotsam salvaged from beaches — while the boarding for sides and roof was plank from the same source, sheathed on the outside with white-cedar shingles, weathered to silvery gray by the salt air.

Such prospect as could be seen from indoors through the small-paned windows was filmed and distorted by the glass, which was ribbed and scoured by sand whipped and driven from the beach in winter gales.

Other than a cast-iron cookstove and the chairs "for company" which Boadicea had borrowed, the furniture was home-made. In the center of this all-purpose room stood a long, rather narrow table flanked by two backless benches. The table top and bench boards were two-inch pine planking and, although they were scarred by various usage, they were holy-stoned to an ivory whiteness — delightful to the touch. The supports of both table and benches were patterned like saw horses, the whole structure being pinned together with removable wooden pegs so that it could be easily knocked down into its component parts.

The entire north end of the room was occupied by two staterooms salvaged from a steamer, as was evidenced by the white-painted paneling, brass door-fittings, and built-in bunks. This arrangement of a cabin within a cabin added to the snugness of this most unusual interior. Unplastered and unsheathed, the house was redolent of cedar, pine, and oak baking in the hot sunshine.

Before we had more than glanced over the room, Boadicea said to the Skipper; "Tha'll please make thysen at hoam in ma' hoose," at the same time relieving him of Jess, whom she put to bed in a clothes basket in which was a pillow stuffed with dried sweetgrass.

"Thank you, we will," replied the Skipper, going toward the entrance door, beside which stood a rough bench with a little pine-staved tub on it and a larger tub of water on the floor below. Beckoning me to join him, he whispered: "Try some fresh water and soap on those hands of yours — blisters heal better without salt in 'em"; and stooping, he dipped up a wooden bailerful of water for me.

When it came to drying my hands on a roller towel hanging handy, I noticed a three-inch wooden trough piercing the wall of the house on an upward slant, the inner end lipping the water tub. Peering through the window, I discovered the other end of the trough hitched to the spout of a small wooden hand pump topping a three-inch iron pipe which sprouted from the sandy ground under the jut of the eaves. Close to the pump was a long bench with a couple of wash tubs thereon and a rubbing board. Boadicea, who had been busy at the stove, must have sensed my interest in this primitive plumbing, for she came over to us to explain.

"Since a' coomed to Noman's there's been no week when a' couldna' attend to ma' bit o' launderin' in th' clear at th'on bench. Father, he drove th'on pipe so deep we'm niver lacked for sweet water at t' pump, come frost or drought. 'Tis a blessin' a' thank ma' Maker for, on ma' bent knees"; and she went back to her cooking.

"The ocean and plenty of clean sand make a good water supply, and the Gulf Stream keeps things warm," was the Skipper's comment.

"But, gosh!" thought I, "how many other women are there who'd bless their Maker if they had to do the weekly washing outdoors in winter!"

The rattling of a wooden latch sent Boadicea to the door to admit young Jethro — the five-year-old son of the house — with a basket of leeks on his arm. Catching sight of the Skipper and me, he looked us over solemnly before a friendly grin lit his tanned face.

"Mind tha' manners, ma' Sonny," cautioned his mother; and he supplemented his smile of approval by sidling up to the Skipper and offering a square, stubby paw, while she added, "An' get tha' oot t' pump to redd up for dinner."

Shortly the boy was back again, his hands a shade less dusky, and a moment later he was sitting between us on one of the long benches showing us his treasures — sharks' eggs, quartz pebbles, a periwinkle spawn, and a ray's stinger, which he fished out of the ample patch-pocket of his blue, faded, home-made overalls.

During the next half-hour Boadicea and the stove conspired to tease my appetite increasingly with a mingle of pleasing odors from kettles and pans. I had just begun to tire of this unfulfilling promise when Sim and Jethro hurried in, all traces of their recent employment scrubbed away.

180

When it came to our places at table, Boadicea arranged the seating: the Skipper on her right, me on her left, Sim opposite me nearest the stove, and Jethro with the boy beside him at the far end of the board. As for Viola — the best-mannered two-year-old imaginable — she sat in her mother's lap with her eyes glued on me, even when opening her mouth for spoonfuls of the clam broth thickened with mashed carrots and cornmeal which Boadicea administered to her.

And presently, when Sim had dealt the plates, beautifully turned of beech wood, smoothed and browned by time — and I had broken through a golden crust of fried batter to discover ivory flakes of codfish that melted on my tongue, bitten into a crisp young leek fresh from the garden patch, sipped coffee of a color and clarity recalling the Island pools, and finally had my share of a big panful of little triangles of crumbly brown pastry filled with wild strawberry preserve, in flavor reminiscent of the spicy uplands whence the berries came — a strange feeling of unreality had come over me. It was as if the curtain of time had been withdrawn, passing me into a fresher, younger age, where one dined simply and intimately with queens, while a snowy-bearded Merlin ministered to one's wants.

A whimper from the baby's basket dispelled this enchantment; but it left the conviction that time is ageless, the present instant its only measure, and that here, in fact, I *was* dining with a queen . . . another Boadicea — who had gained her crown and the allegiance of her subjects, not by prerogative, but by virtue of her sex, the splendor of her person, and the nobility of her character — with the historic result that her realm prospered and was content.

"And now, old man," said the Skipper, looking at me, "tell 'em your tale of the boot on Cuttyhunk" — which in due course I did, under a raking crossfire of questions from Sim and Jethro, while Boadicea sat rigid, her face paling and flushing as the evidence linked with our find her own shipwreck and rescue.

And it was she who brought the session to an end by leaving her seat to drop Viola on Jethro's lap, lift Jess out of her basket, unhook a long brass key from a peg beside the door, and, turning to face us, exclaim:

"Tha'll all please t' coom wi' me to th'on Town Hoose!" — at the same time holding the door open for us to pass outside and take the path through the village.

It was during our short walk to the white building that Boadicea registered the first and only note of discontent, when she said, "Ah'm thinkin' sometimes th'on preacher might coom here, as 'e was wont — tho' we'm alone now by oursens. Ah'm no hand wi' prayers an' t' Scriptures, an' as for ma' dear lad an' Father, they can do nowt wi' 'em."

The "Town House" we were approaching was, in fact, church, school, and forum, all in one, and a strikingly well-proportioned pocket edition of the best in New England meeting house architecture. Based on a low underpinning of dressed granite, with a broad, shallow step of the same material leading to a portico from which rose two Ionic columns supporting a pediment, the front, facing south, had all the charm lent by such classic details. A plain but graceful small belfry capped the pediment, breaking the ridge line of the roof. In each of the long sides were two tall windows, with louvered blinds painted dark green to relieve the monotony of white, clapboarded siding.

Coming to the door, Boadicea, after unlocking it and swinging it open, waved us in. A dais at the north end with a table on it faced rows of wooden benches filling the otherwise unfurnished room. These benches were unique, inasmuch as they were so constructed that they could be sat on with comfort by grown-ups — or, by reversing the function of the footrests, could be converted into seats and desks for children.

But transcending these physical aspects was the awesome impression of the building when one thought of the lives and circumstances of the builders. For a small community of squat-

182

ters to tax its time, labor, and meager purse to establish and maintain such an institution was an almost unprecedented example of faith, courage, and aspiration. It was hallowed ground indeed, and I bowed my head in reverence when we were seated on one of the benches, while Boadicea, who had mounted the dais, stood facing us with Jess on her arm.

For a moment or two she stood silent, looking upward for her inspiration. Then slowly, but without hesitation or fumbling, she poured out her prayer for the welfare of "th' lads in th'on lifeboat," who had risked and lost their lives in their effort to save hers. Her utter unconsciousness of self had the effect of transmuting her homespun appeal to uplifting eloquence, wafting our spirits with hers to the Heaven in which she had such simple, boundless faith.

And as we came out again into the sunshine to halt for a moment while Boadicea closed and locked the door, I was conscious of her power to hold the loyalty and affection of her subjects — Jethro and Sim — and all others who, like the Skipper and me, might come within her influence.

Coming down the step to join us she announced, "Ah'm thinkin' Tuesda'll be movin' day"; and in answer to our blank looks of surprise, "Ah'm uneasy bidin' long in one hoose wi' so many idle ones aboot — all wishful to be lived in."

And demonstrating this most unusual point of view with an assessment of the good and bad features of the unoccupied cabins, she gradually involved Sim and Jethro in the discussion, implicating them in her plans with such simple guile that it was not long before they proposed we should all take a look around.

Of the lot, five were ruinous — "fit only for kindlin's"; while the others, as compared with "th'on of ours," seemed to me conspicuously lacking in any detail which could appeal to such a housewife as Boadicea. But to her gladsome eye none was without special charm, with the result that the whole dilapidation acquired a vitality; so that, when we had finished our inspection and come to the last dip in the path on our way down to the landing beach, I stopped in my tracks to take one more look at the village — with no sense of depression, but rather one of firm assurance that, though derelict, it was still alive.

It was here on the bluff's top that the Skipper and I regretfully said goodbye to Boadicea and her children; while Sim and Jethro went on ahead down to the fish house, to join us presently on the beach, present us with a box of salt cod, and lend us a hand in launching the *Peapod*. As we started paddling out to the *Fox,* Sim standing barefoot in the shallows, called out:

"Them ducks'll be nestin' over yonder on the hill come springtime, Skipper, even if I ain't here. Better come over an' have a look at 'em!" — and then he waded ashore to follow Jethro into the fish house to bait trawl, and to leave in my memory as a last picture of Sim a shock of silvery hair, a wisp of white beard blown off a shoulder, and a great, giant back stooped to pass under a low door lintel. For when that next springtime came, Sim's long trick at the helm was over.

It was perhaps twenty minutes later, with the *Fox,* underway and heading homeward, sailing under the steep-to bluff where we had left Boadicea, that I looked up over my shoulder to see her standing on the crest above us — her face and uncovered head aglow in the rays of the westering sun.

As I waved my hat in a final farewell, she raised her left arm with Jess aloft, and threw out her right in a spacious gesture as if bidding us Godspeed on some gallant venture — leaving me then, and now, to ponder the enigma of a spirit of such limitless influence as hers at work in a sphere so inconsiderable and unconsidered as to be in fact as well as in name — Noman's.

FOURTEEN

Holly Days

A LATE-RISING December sun was shaping above a rosy mist that smoked up from a land drenched by yesterday's warm southwester. Poking my head out of my ivy-framed window at The Cottage I snuffed the cool freshness of dawn, redolent with the odor of wet fallen leaves. Beyond a vividly green field of winter rye the bare branches of a beech clump were etched against the glowing eastern sky. The clangor of a flock of crows in a nearby pine assured good weather for the Christmas oystering.

By ten o'clock that morning the wheels of the wide-track white wagon had rattled the planks of the old Padanaram Bridge with the ebb tide swirling noisily below, and the Skipper had eased Box and Cox, the roan pair, up the long Gulf Hill, tooled us at a brisk pace across the Bakerville Ridge, and after several miles of tortuous, sandy farm lanes brought us to a barway in a wall. Beyond this we jolted and rocked over a quarter-mile of plow and stony pasture to a pebbly reach on the east shore of the estuary known as Pascamanset River. The horses were blanketed and hitched in the lee of a stand of upland cedars. Then Willie, Levi, and I, with our gear of gum boots, gunny sacks, and light hammers, were herded to the water's edge by the Skipper, who must have noticed my disgracefully chapped hands, for as I started to draw on some cotton gloves before wading he said:

"Leave those gloves of yours ashore and let the salt water work into your cracked hands. I'll guarantee if you'll grin and bear it today you'll cure 'em for good and all." And he was right, for his cure has lasted without a break — fifty-eight years.

Stern to the beach, where the Skipper stood directing operations, I could let the tears flow without loss of face, as stooping over I grubbed among the infernally sharp-shelled oysters, elbow deep in the cold water. I soon found there was a tricky art in knocking a cluster away from its stone anchorage without smashing its tough but brittle armor, and, although I kept at it steadily until my back ached and my hands were cut to ribands, my sack, after an hour, looked pitifully lean as it dragged beside me.

"Keep working downstream — not up," the Skipper warned as we three (Levi, the biggest, well out beyond me, with Willie between us) stooped and stumbled among the weedy shingle. "The oysters above here have too much fresh water and color in 'em for Christmas eating," he ended.

By noon the bags bulged and we were ordered ashore to a spot above high-water mark where a broken bank sheltered us from the breath of north wind that sighed through the fronds of the junipers above. Here the sun lay warm and the little fire of driftwood that we kindled burned steadily without blowing about, quickly heating the circle of stones we ranged round it.

When the fire died to a bed of glowing embers and the stones shimmered, we broached a little of our cargo of oysters and set them to roasting. And when, a few minutes later, the Skipper remarked, "The harder they come, the sweeter they chew," I sensed there was indeed a special seasoning in the dozen or so of fat, salty morsels I was savoring. Our drink, I remember, was smoky China tea from pint bottles wrapped in heavy woolen socks — still piping hot after the journey; and this, with slabs of sweet, pale-yellow Adamsville cheese and wedges of apple pie gave us, I thought, an ideally balanced ration.

Later in the afternoon, farther downstream, in a little land of wooden hillocks that pushed up abruptly from the marshy margin of the river, we came to a mysterious bower. Old and young, large and small, this lovely stand of holly trees, blazing here and there with clusters of red berries, jinked and glittered as the level rays of the westering sun were caught for an instant by the luster of the evergreen leaves. And here with care for shape and future growth, we pruned the sprigs and sprays for our Christmas "trimmery." Before we finished, the Skipper found on the underside of a single leaf on a holly sapling a tiny golden bat, hung up for the winter. The leaf he'd chosen for his long sleep stood with the side to which he was hooked faced south to the noonday sun, while the tougher topside of the leaf shielded him from the cold north. When we tickled his belly with a twig he squeaked and bared his needle-pointed teeth — so, wishing this Scrooge a Merry Christmas, we left him and lugged our prickly spoil out to the wagon.

The drive home in the chilly dusk by way of Smith's Neck was spiced at its start by the fording of Little River — a small sister of Pascamanset. As we came to the middle, the strong flood tide boiled and foamed over the hubs and into the bed of the wagon. Box and Cox snorted and floundered and there came a moment when we rocked perilously on the edge of disaster. Here the Skipper by skillful use of voice, whip, and reins yanked us out on the farther bank in a scutter of stones and shower of spray. Two hours later, as we toiled up the sharp pitch of the home driveway, the dancing reflection of red fire-light on dining-room windowpanes was a welcome sight to me, a tired and shivery young mouse.

Filled with such preparations, the days of December had run toward the twenty-fifth — every one with its time-established job of work, planned and ordered.

There had been Turkey Day — a long one — when we had driven to a distant shore farm, reached through a succession of barways, where on the salt meadows a flock of big fowls grew plump and sweet on a diet of fiddler crabs. Here the Skipper had chosen a fine white bird for the "boiler" and a busting bronze one for the "roaster," and we had brought them home to be slain, plucked, drawn, and hung.

Then there had been Meal Day, when we had hauled our own-grown corn on the cob to Russell's Mills and returned with our bag of meal, cool ground by the slow-turning stones and in prime condition for Deborah, the cook, to work up into her incomparably rich Christmas dumplings.

On the soft, gray rainy days there had been mince to be chopped for pies, and party silver and glass to be polished. The long evenings had been spent in the gun room with the Skipper, helping to rig a pair of model sailboats for a brace of cousins expected for the holiday.

And then at last had come the twenty-third — Carriage House Day — when that dark, barn-like building was cleared of the wagons and lumber and warmed and "cosied" by two big wood-burning stoves, a long table, chairs, and the sundry properties for a feast, and finally was decked and made gay with sprays of holly and fans and wreaths of sage-green dusty miller — true emblems of our December weather.

Ever since Thanksgiving the Skipper's last rite before bed-time had been the inspection of a stone crock that stood in the cool, damp cellar. The contents — Barbados rum, French brandy, lemons, and preserved peaches — would be gently stirred with a wand of sassafras, and a glass "thief" full of it would be held to the candlelight to make sure the fruit was being proper-ly consumed by and blended with the liquor. A little sip from the thief that evening gave assurance that the "Cottage Punch" had come on nicely.

Christmas Eve — and we of that household in hard training from the preceding days were in tune with the spiritual significance of the Holy Festival. Looking back, I'm sure the Skipper approached this celebration as an ardent but thoughtful bridegroom comes to his wedding — "not . . . lightly; but reverently . . . and in the fear of God"; and from this approach of his have sprung my evergreen memories of those winter times — unnipped by the snow and frost, wariness and surfeit, of a later custom. What did we care if next day were fair or foul; we were "swept and garnished" within and without, orderly prepared to give of our plenty to our neighbors and to one another.

This year Christmas Day was fair — mildly cold and clear — with a heavy white frost covering the fields, which later, under the influence of brilliant sunshine, was magicked into a myriad of tiny rainbow jewels that sparkled for a moment and were gone, leaving the grass refreshed and vivid. A Bristol County Christmas indeed, and one to spur us to our best performance!

By nine in the morning we had the oysters shucked, the punch, tempered and blended with black India tea, chilling in a corner of the well house, fires kindled in the carriage house and fuel for the day beside 'em, the chairs dusted, the long table set, the cranberries for garnish polished and strung; and were finally ready to face, with cheerful fortitude, our great ordeal — Deborah's tindery temper that we suspected would be darting about the farmhouse like forked lightning when we came to help her with the last touches for the family dinner and the neighborhood dance and supper which were to follow. Our anticipations were realized, for the changes she rang on "clumsy" were a revelation.

On the tick of two-thirty the Skipper, in navy-blue broadcloth, a sprig of holly with red berries in his buttonhole, entered the carriage house, "Friend Rachel," our loved and lovely Quaker aunt, on his arm. Suiting his pace to her age, he escorted her to a chair at the end of the long table, facing the door. Here she sat, her pearl-gray habit and snowy little house-cap all a-shimmer in the yellow light of four candelabra that were ranged symmetrically on the cream-colored damask tablecloth.

After this little ceremony the Skipper stood by his chair at the head of the table, ready to greet the rest of us as we came in and took our seats. Silence fell for a moment as with bowed heads we offered thanks to Heaven for what we were to receive. Followed a slight "chump!" as the Skipper drove his carving fork into the crackling brown breast of the roaster that lay before him, laced with chaplets of crimson cranberries. Aunt Rachel, at her end, carved the boiler with graceful dexterity. My choice then and ever since has been the boiled with plenty of oyster sauce — but tastes differ, and many preferred the roast with pounded chestnut stuffing seasoned with sage and onion.

Of course there was mashed Nantucket turnip, white and delicate as driven snow; there were dumplings of gray cornmeal — suggesting blanched almonds, only better; tapering columns of cranberry jelly — glowing rubies, tart and frosty; stalks of bleached celery — brittle as ice — full of the savor of rich black soil.

But long before our appetites were dulled the Skipper caught my eye — a prearranged signal that set five girls and boys to clearing the table for dessert. After the flurry of this office I led my band to the scullery to lend a hand with the pudding and a Chinese-red tray of fruit. Heading the procession on our return marched Deborah in a print gown of startling shade and pattern. The pudding, her masterpiece, tricked with holly and so ethereal that the raisins and chopped nuts, the suet and the spices, seemed held together by brown gossamer, was set all glistening before the Skipper, while its proud creator took her seat at his right hand to ladle out the cinnamon-flavored, creamy sauce from a silver boat. The tray, with its pyramid of pale-green Beurre d'Anjou pears and stalks of hothouse grapes the color of amethysts, spread fruitful good tidings from the center of the table. The Skipper poured a generous glassful of brandy over the pudding, the candles were extinguished, the Skipper scratched a match — and we sat dimly revealed by the gold and blue flames of the blazing spirits.

A few minutes after midnight, when Walter, the accordion player, had called the numbers in the last dance, when the yellow-capped baking dishes of scalloped oysters laced with sherry and reinforced with mince pies had been exhausted and the punch bowl had been filled and emptied for the last time, Levi, who was helping me put the lamps in the carriage house, neatly balled the yarns of our Christmas Day by remarking:

"I guess it ain't the cut o' the jib that counts so much as the way you trim it!"

YANKEE • CLASSICS

IN THIS exciting new series, Yankee Books brings back into print rare classics of New England literature that previously have commanded the highest prices as rare books if and when they could be found. The editors have selected only those titles that are as lively and enthralling to today's reading audience as they were to that of a generation ago.